The Art Beat

By
Alan Klevit

Llumina Press

Requests for permission to make copies of any part of this work should be mailed to Permissions Department, Llumina Press, PO Box 772246, Coral Springs, FL 33077-2246

ISBN: 1-932303-39-1
Printed in the United States of America

Dedicated to Katie, Anna and Daniel
Who give me unconditional love
And hope for the future

For Michael + Lia —
Thanks for the "coming out"
party. Mostly, thanks
for your friendship.

Alan.

Table of Contents

Acknowledgements

*I*f my daughter, Mindy, did not attend art school, I would not have ended up in the art business. My former wife and partner, Marilyn, and I bought our first art gallery, with the thought that "it belonged to Mindy." So thanks, Mindy, for your interest in art and your enthusiasm for it, which eventually reawakened my interest, which had been dormant for so many years.

I enjoyed going to museums with Mindy, accompanying her class, listening to docents and professors, and expanding my understanding and appreciation of art because of her unique insights. When we opened our gallery in Gaithersburg, Maryland, she worked part time until she completed art studies at the Maryland School of Art & Design, when she took over full time. While I coached her in the art of selling, she continued my education in art appreciation. I also watched her create her art and learned about techniques in various mediums. No one else has ever displayed such fervor for the arts as you, Mindy. My gratitude is boundless.

Some of my favorite artists helped my education, too. I am grateful to all of them and appreciate their friendship.

Ivan Dobroruka's art was, according to one critic, "Dali with a Byzantine twist." Ivan's passion for the arts enabled him to interpret music through his paintings and etchings. He also illustrated Shakespeare's sonnets. A friend of immense talent and sensitivity, I will never forget the night he gave Mindy a lesson in draftsmanship at my Malibu home. It is more than a coincidence that "dobroruka" means good hands in Czech. Dobroruka was born in Prague, and is represented in that city's prestigious museum. Sadly, Ivan is no longer with us.

Sitting on the floor and watching & helping Elaine Burch print her etchings and aquatints was invaluable training. I was happy for her when UNESCO selected two of her images to be made into cards for worldwide distribution to raise money for hungry children around the globe.

Tadeusz Lapinski, recognized as one of the foremost print makers of the 20th century, generously shared his studio and time with me, and patiently explained his special technique in lithography. Tad's masterpieces are in the collections of more than a hundred important museums, many of which have held exhibitions of his works.

Carol Kucera showed me various ways to paint. She used everything from brushes to spatulas to coke bottles to apply paint--and we spent hours talking about art and her style. She brought a lyricism to her work, incorporating her talent as a poet and musician. I was pleased when NASA selected her to paint several pieces for their museum, chronicling Sally Ride's ride, and they even included one of Carol's poems in their initial exhibition of that event.

Ed Dwight was more than a sculptor [and former astronaut]. Ed ran his own foundry. We became friends and he spent hours with me, explaining how a bronze evolves from a wax model, and can be repeated in a multiple edition. The *Frederick Douglass* sculpture at Harper's Ferry, W. Va., is by Ed, along with more than fifty other statues of famous Americans, including Dr. Martin Luther King, George Washington Carver, Harriet Tubman, Hank Aaron, and the Kunta Kinte–Alex Haley memorial. Ed taught sculpture and art history at the University of Denver, ran their metal sculpture foundry, and has become an internationally acclaimed sculptor.

Every major contemporary museum in the world includes works by Yaacov Agam in their collections. Yaacov spent hours with me, explaining his work, his philosophy, and the transformation from the creative spark to a drawing on paper, to a major work of art, such as the fire & water sculpture in front of the United Nations building at Lake Success or the Interplay sculpture in front of the Lincoln Center. Agam is the first artist I interviewed for television.

I appreciate several art dealers, who shared their knowledge with me over the years. The late Lee Silberstein [Georgetown Graphics in Washington, D. C.] comes to mind. We spent many mornings discussing art over an espresso and croissant at a coffee shop across from his gallery. Another mentor was Rashad Hopkins of Bowles-Hopkins in San Francisco. Rashad was instrumental in the transformation of my galleries to among D. C.'s finest. Two of my closest personal friends, Andrew Weiss and Fred Laidlaw, have been fine art dealers for decades, and my nearly daily conversations with them over the years have greatly broadened my understanding of art and the art business. Andy and I go back twenty-seven years, Fred and I about ten. Thanks, guys. I hope you've gained something, too. Several close friends in the music world have expanded my view and understanding of art— and the relationship between the arts. Thanks to Lori Barth, Ernie Watts, Bob Leatherbarrow and the late Pete Bardens.

Paul Ruffman deserves mention for his unwavering support, loyalty and friendship. I am grateful for his inviting me to write for his publications, the latest and current one being *The Malibu Chronicle.*

Special thanks to Marilyn Klevit, who worked tirelessly with me as we grew a dream into a major art business, which opened the opportunities for me to learn about art from perspectives that would otherwise not have been available. And thanks for giving me the space to pursue my writing in the first place.

And there is Patty, who never ceases to believe in me as a writer. Your encouragement and continuous support, as well as your invaluable editing and suggestions, are paramount in my pursuing this career. Thank you, my love.

Finally, I offer my gratitude to artists in all the arts, most of whom create in anonymity, and who bring beauty and joy to the world, raise our level of consciousness, and make this planet a worthwhile place to live, despite everything else going on in it. Vincent Price, on his deathbed, said it best, when assured by friends he was going to heaven: *"If there is no art there, I don't have to go."*

Bravo, Vincent.

Foreword

I first met Alan Klevit in the early 1990's. We were introduced by Peter Bardens, a close friend of each of us. Pete was a fellow Englishman and renowned musician who had appeared as a guest several times on Alan's television show. Alan's interviews with Pete were entertaining, sometimes hilarious. They also demonstrated his knowledge and insight into music. That was all the more remarkable, because his background, I later learned, was in the world of fine art, where he had an international reputation. Alan's guests covered all the arts, from writers and poets, to movie directors, actors, musicians, art dealers, architects, photographers, and producers. His breadth of knowledge has always impressed me.

Alan was also a writer, and when I created and published MALIBU MAGAZINE, at my urging, he became a regular contributor, and his short stories were a popular feature in the magazine. He eventually shifted the focus of his writing to coincide with his television show, which was extremely popular in the Malibu Area, and emphasized discussions about the arts. His popularity grew, as readers found his columns educational, provocative and filled with an acerbic wit.

As publisher of the MALIBU CHRONICLE, I continued to print Alan's column, *The Art Beat*, which is a favorite among our readers. Personally, I have learned a great deal about art from him. He not only possesses a great understanding about art and its role our society and the political issues which surround it, he has an intimate knowledge of the creative aspects of art, and the various mediums used to create it. He also knows the workings of the art business and offers valuable advice to people who would be collectors.

Alan and I have become close friends over the years, and I value his friendship and his integrity as much as the contribution he has made to my publications over the years. Congratulations for buying this compilation. You are in for a real treat.

Paul Ruffman
Publisher, THE MALIBU CHRONICLE

Background

Welcome to my world of art. Over the past three decades, I have been an art collector, dealer, publisher, gallery operator, artist's agent, corporate art consultant, TV talk show host, and auctioneer, often all at once. I have held season tickets to the theater, the opera and the philharmonic, and attended performances from coast to coast and across the pond. Two words summarize all of these hats: Art Lover! I cannot imagine my life without art in it.

My exposure to the world of art has its roots in the 1940's. I lived in Washington, D. C., in the "ghetto" in Southwest. It was one of the poorer parts of the city, chock full of minority groups and first and second generation immigrant families. At the same time, most of the city's museums were a stone's throw away. A brisk twenty minute walk, and I could be at the Smithsonian, with its array of museums, or the Mellon Art Gallery, which later became known as the National Gallery of Art. The Phillips Collection, with its extraordinary Impressionist collection, the Renwick, the Freer and a few others were not much farther. These are not just local city museums. They are world class museums.

The proximity of the museums would not have mattered had it not been for the opportunity to visit them. Since our family was Orthodox Jewish, we observed an abundance of holidays, not just the High Holy Days of Rosh Hashonna and Yom Kippur. I went to Synagogue instead of school on the first two days of Passover, the first two days of Chanukah, the first two and last two days of Succoth, Purim, and a handful of lessor-known holidays, even among a majority of the Jewish population. Generally speaking, services lasted until about eleven. After lunch, a group of us would walk to the museums. From the age of eight or nine until my mid teens, I visited museums at least a dozen times a year, which means more than seventy visits during some very impressionable years. Most people do not visit museums that often in their lifetime. The truth is, my annual visits to museums has averaged less than half a dozen in recent years. When I visit Europe, the number goes up slightly.

By the time I entered high school, I could give my impressions of works of Van Gogh, Renoir, Manet, Monet, Degas, Cezanne, Goya, Dali, Remington, Russell, Bellows, early Americans whose names are less known, numerous Dutch Masters, and a litany of Renaissance and other European masters. As my interest in art piqued, I began reading about artists as a youngster, learning about their lives even as I enjoyed their art.

For me, art is more than something pretty to look at and admire. As a kid, I looked forward to those treks to the museums. It was as though I was getting my fix. I became hooked on art. Emotionally involved. And that passion has grown the past fifty years.

More than an emotional involvement, art became somewhat of a refuge. The museums were a hiding place, if you will, from poverty, prejudice and World War II. It occurred to me in my very formative years, that art was therapeutic. Today, that has become common knowledge, and colleges offer degrees in art therapy. I also hid in the pictures I saw, burying myself in my favorite scenes, becoming part of the art, surrounding myself in the time and place. I recognize that, subliminally, even as a boy I understood that art was a reflection of society, and those masterpieces offered me refuge in a time gone by.

I was also spiritually engulfed by the religious art that abounded. Since the religion depicted in all the great paintings was Christianity, you might wonder how it could have an effect on a Jewish kid. It did. Many years later, I understood why. It was when I gazed upon the *Pieta* at the world's fair in New York in 1964. Standing on a moving platform, having waited two hours with my wife and three children, ages 7, 4 and one, I moved by it in two and a half minutes, and felt chills and shivers all over. I got back in line at the Vatican Exhibit and waited an additional two hours for another two-minute fix. Michelangelo's simple, luminous marble of Mary holding her dead son in her lap touched my soul. It regenerated my own religious beliefs.

That is when I recognized another role that art plays in our lives. You will find out what that role is when you read the column, *They Touch my Soul*, which is included in this book. With that childhood foundation, it is little wonder that, while teaching in Charlottesville, Virginia some twenty years later, I frequented an art gallery across the street from the University of Virginia's main campus, directly opposite those serpentine walls designed by Thomas Jefferson. There I saw and bought my first works of art: original lithographs by Marc Chagall, Fernand Leger and Pierre Bonnard. One of the columns included in this collection explains what a lithograph is and what makes it original.

So that is how it all began. It was not an accident that I ended up in the art business in 1974. I needed to be around art. Although that first gallery was bought for my daughter, Mindy, I hung out there all the time. I knew nothing about the business, but loved being surrounded by the art..

Given the opportunity to roam about the art, to see it up close, to touch it, I became completely hooked and immersed myself in the world of art. It was not enough running a gallery. Within seven months, we opened a second one. Then a third, our "flagship" gallery that was larger than the other two combined. And more elegant. Four separate salons with original art by twentieth century masters and emerging artists we represented. Finally, I opened a fourth gallery, with my friend, Andy Weiss.

I needed more. I wasn't satisfied with a passive role in art. I needed to watch artists paint, watch them create their lithographs, etchings and serigraphs, sketch, create clay models for sculptures. I talked to them, questioned them, so I could understand what motivated them and what was the source of their creativity, and attained practical knowledge about how art works are made. I even helped a few print their lithographs and etchings.

For twenty-seven years, I grew with my business. I learned that, just as art has mirrored society and recorded where we have been as a civilization, there are artists who anticipate the world of tomorrow. In all of the arts, yesterday's science fiction has become today's reality. From Da Vinci's laser beams, submarines and helicopters, to Jules Verne, Buck Rogers, Arthur Clarke, Isaac

Asimov, and Ray Bradbury, to name a few, we are introduced to the world of tomorrow. *What He Saw Is What We Got* addresses that notion. Other artists simply want to get our attention, engage and interact with us for a moment, getting us to stop and reflect on the beauty which abounds around us.

I am sure of this: The role of art is intact. Undeniable. Which is why it must be preserved. And why artists must be allowed to "go where no man has gone before." Stifle creativity in the name of taste, censorship, religion, or anything else, and we may well be stifling the development of man. There are probably more columns on this general issue than any other.

I began writing what I learned from artists. I also wrote about the artists themselves. A local paper began printing my views and some major art magazines printed anecdotal stories and biographies I wrote about some of my favorite artists. A local radio station began airing my views on art a few times a week. I wrote a book on another subject and ended up promoting it on television.

Then, after twenty years in the art world, came the opportunity to host a television show in Southern California. Everything I had done until that moment had prepared me for this show.

I immediately shifted gears. I interviewed known and emerging artists. Other guests included art dealers, writers, and critics. It was a freewheeling, no-holds-barred talk show, recorded live and presented to viewers throughout the Los Angeles Area without editing. We talked about everything from art history to the Masters, to the role of art in society and art appreciation. The most heated discussions ensued when the topics were social and political issues such as censorship and government funding.

Eventually, I expanded my guest list to include people from other art mediums, including authors, actors, musicians, directors, stunt men and women, architects, designers, poets, et al. The show changed names a few times, but eventually became *The Art Beat*. Throughout the six and a half years the show aired, every month or so I would not schedule a guest. The first time, my guest was unable to show at the last minute. Rather than cancel the show, I decided to take the opportunity to talk to my viewers. I shared a few humorous stories about several famous artists. [Years later, my story about Salvador Dali became a popular column and is included in this book.] I decided to use the show as a platform for me to express my opinions and concerns about the art world, the role of art in society and other topics of interest. I brought etching plates and works of art to the studio and taught people how original graphics are made and how to tell fakes from originals.

Educating people about art, offering advice on collecting art, tips on how to develop a broader appreciation for all the arts, well, these were my favorite shows. They were the inspiration for my column, *The Art Beat*.

The column first appeared on a regular basis in MALIBU MAGAZINE in 1996, and eventually wound up in THE MALIBU CHRONICLE. It has also appeared in several e-magazines and other newspapers on a non-regular basis.

I want to share my experiences in art with the widest possible audience. I want you to appreciate it as much as I do, to be nurtured by it, if you are not already. If you aren't, I hope to provide an insight and perspective to help you do that. I also hope to encourage and motivate you to fight to keep art programs in schools, so our children have the same opportunity to benefit from it as I did. I want you to cajole and stand up to those who would deny its natural paths, in the name of whatever euphemism or pseudonym they substitute for censorship. I want you to get as angry as I do, when someone gets up on the floor of Congress and decries public television as 'elitist.' Since when is education elitist? I also want to share my experiences in collecting art, providing useful information from my insider's view, with the aim of preventing novice or experienced collectors from being burned.

Thanks for your interest in the arts. Please take the time to visit a museum in the next few weeks. Or attend a concert or a play. And watch something on public television. Of course, include a kid in your experience.

Preface

H ow does one decide which columns to put in a compilation? It's not like the decision could be based on sales, like a pop singer's golden oldies. It's more like a self-proclaimed expert putting together a compilation of *Puccini's Greatest Arias*. A lot of personal taste goes into that sort of thing.

One dilemma in eliminating any column is that I wrote them all. They are all part of me, extensions of my mind and soul. I recall several artists telling me that, at first, it was difficult for them to sell any of their art. As the painter Carol Kucera put it, "They are my children. I love them all. I don't want to lose any."

These are the criteria I used in selecting what is in and what is out. Basically, this compilation includes my favorites and those columns that drew the most reaction from readers, perhaps a dozen of those. That does not necessarily mean positive reaction. For example, the columns that dealt with censorship elicited the greatest response. They also were the most controversial, with about 75-25 pro versus con for the *Hooray for Mikey* column, and 60-40 for the *C'mon Rudy* piece. Rudy Giuliani was a popular mayor, so my criticism of him elicited some nasty comments from readers.

Lots of readers complained about my list of the top ten artists of the century. As for my four favorite works of art in the world, some readers asked me if I were blind or crazy. "Where is Michelangelo's David?" was the most frequent question and demand on that topic.

The second criterion I applied to my selection process was how useful a column might be to you, the reader. *Don't Buy Art at a Yard Sale* and *Are You Kidding, Sotheby's?* typify columns that fit that bill. I want art collectors to be as knowledgeable as possible when they are out there in the marketplace, at the mercy of people who want to sell them art under the caveat, "buyer beware."

I included columns in which I complained about our society as it relates to the arts, and others that might serve as catalysts for people new to the arts, in the hope that they will be turned on to the joy of art appreciation. I also included some of my favorite anecdotal stories about important artists. *The Old Man and the Sea* is a personal favorite, while more readers liked *Hello, Dali!*

The purpose of my column is not just to inform readers about art, although I try to do that. It is not solely to educate, although I attempt to do that, too. It is not to entertain, although I certainly take a stab at that as well. My purpose is to tweak you into wanting to make the arts more important to you and your family. That is equally true if you are already an avid art lover or a neophyte. Art is boundless, its potential for increasing the value of our lives infinite. As you read the columns, you will discover my passion for the arts. I hope that I can arouse yours. Let me know. Don't hesitate to comment about them and ask questions they raise or don't cover. Tell me what you like and don't like, and any aspect of art you would like me to consider for a future column. Email me at theartbeat@charter.net.

The second part of this book contains frequently asked questions I have been asked on my show, through my column and various internet avenues, where I volunteer as an 'art expert.' I have selected those which could be of value to art collectors, experienced or neophyte, art lovers, and perhaps cultural anthropologists who are just plain curious.

What it comes down to is that *The Art Beat* is a combination of Art Appreciation 101, Art History 202, Art & Society 303, My Favorite Artists 404, and some personal gripes and views that don't fit anywhere.

For me the arts are all the same. I especially like to intertwine visual art and music, not unlike the movie director who recognizes the importance of marrying a great score to equally great cinematography. And of course, a good story helps!

Alan Klevit
Malibu, California

The Soul of Art

What makes an artist tick? Several columns cover the lives of artists and examine their creative spirits. Others reflect on the esoteric qualities and benefits of art, and how the author has personalized and used them in his life.

They Touch My Soul

I occasionally get together with some friends to discuss music, art, theater, and other creative arts. My announcing my favorite works of art in Europe prompted one of our more heated debates. Since my friends are European transplants, I suspect nationalistic pride influenced their choices. Here are my favorites:

On the outskirts of Oslo, Norway, is the Vigeland Museum, an outdoor museum in a park setting, with a remarkable array of sculptures by Gustav Vigeland [1869-1943]. There are 192 life-size works in stone and bronze, sometimes roughly hewn, often smooth, depicting the human condition, modeled in full size. The sculptures portray people of all ages at work and play, happy and unhappy, expressing relationships between men & women and adults & children, including the unusual theme of the father-child relationship. Almost primitive, reminiscent of Intuit carvings, somewhat Picasso-esque [Vigeland is often referred to as *Picasso of the North*], these stark works are emotionally wrenching with their contrasting pathos and tenderness. They are powerful, elegant and hopeful renderings of men, women and children from birth to death. I spent three days wandering around the park, smiling back at the statues, crying with them, touching them, and talking to them. They may be bronze and cold stone, but their hearts are warm and alive, as they represent, with deceptive simplicity, Man's struggle for existence.

St. Petersburg, Russia is a shrine to a time gone by. The manicured lawns of the countryside complement its golden domes and 18th & 19th century baroque & neoclassical structures. Spread over more than 100 islands and criss-crossed by more than sixty rivers and canals, St. Petersburg is known as the Venice of the North. [What's with those people who think everything great began in the South of Europe?] Catherine's Summer Palace is the city's jewel, the last vestige of the opulent days of imperialism. Designed by Bartomoleo Rastrelli, who brought Italian flair to the

Byzantine design, it has a magnificent aqua colored facade, decorated with noble statues, encrusted with gold and white ornaments and topped with gold onion domes. Inside, everything is quintessential Russian: colorful, highly stylized and ornate, from Baroque to art deco. There are paintings of religious icons with hand-carved gilded frames; chandeliers and candelabras dripping with crystal; a dining room filled with a wood inlaid table and twenty-six high-backed chairs with plush silk seats and backs, which surround the table like thrones. On the table are finely cut crystal goblets, translucent china with hand-painted cobalt blue and 22k gold designs, eggs by Faberge, and solid gold cutlery. I find the palace romantic and sexy with its not-quite-over-the-top opulence.

The unfinished Cathedral de Familia by Antoni Gaudi is the Grande Dame of Barcelona. Designed to pay homage to the Creator, its spires appear to be living creatures that bend and shoot toward the heavens. They remind me of pelicans when they elongate their bodies and dive-bomb into the ocean. The spires are spear-like sculptures tightly packed together with enough space between them to allow the viewer to get a peek inside, but shadows hide the view. Standing in front of it, I felt as though I were in the presence of a living object. Gaudi died before its completion. The story behind his death adds to the cathedral's mystique. Gaudi worked without blueprints, visualizing his masterpiece as it took shape, and personally directing its construction. One day he stepped back to admire his work, and a bus ran over and killed him! The final structure, which lived in Gaudi's head, died with him. Now, more than seventy years later, construction is underway to complete the cathedral, based on what present-day architects think Gaudi wanted the final structure to be. This great Cathedral is one of the aesthetic wonders of the world. When I see it from afar, my heart beats a little faster. Up close, I am mesmerized and drawn into its web.

Rome is the Eternal City. From the Pantheon, the most perfect of the ancient monuments, its great dome an engineering and artistic marvel; to the Coliseum, its architectural genius intact; from its great fountains to its monumental sculptures; Rome lives through the eyes and hands of Michelangelo, Bernini, Bramante, Caravaggio, and Raphael. My favorite is a simple marble figure in St. Peter's Basilica. I first saw it in 1964 in New York, after my wife, our three children [ages 1, 4 & seven] and I waited two hours for a two and a half-minute glance. Then I stood in line another two hours for a second glimpse of Michelangelo's *Pieta*. It was worth it. I visualized Michelangelo carving into the marble block, his love and hope pouring through his hands into the cold stone, smoothing out the figure of the Virgin Mary holding the body of Christ, bringing life to his creation with his fingers, as God did to man in Michelangelo's painting of creation in the ceiling of the Sistine Chapel. I have visited *Pieta* many times. Its power is intact; it continues to evoke a response from me, as it has touched others for centuries. It is more beautiful with each visit, its already rich patina more lustrous, as though God has infused it with His Special Light, much as He whispered His Ninth Symphony to the deaf Beethoven.

The common denominator shared by Vigeland's figures, Catherine's Palace, Gaudi's Cathedral, and Michelangelo's *Pieta* is their ability to touch my soul. I would not own any work of art that did not touch me. Neither should you. Art should harmonize with your soul, not your sofa.

The Old Man and the Sea

*I*n the summer of 1968 I rented a villa on the Southern Coast of Spain. Every afternoon I would walk along the shoreline, enjoying both the sunrise and the sunset on the water. One afternoon, as the sun began its descent, I saw the silhouette of a man less than a hundred yards away.

He returned my wave, and we met at the water's edge. He was slightly shorter than I, bald, stockily built, well tanned, and with riveting coal-like eyes. *Buenes tardes,* I said in my best Spanish accent. *Good evening,* he replied, in a better English accent.

I watched him doodle in the sand. He was sure of himself, drawing with a stick at an amazing speed, creating figures as fast as the incoming tide washed away what he had done. His figures were deceptively simple, as he drew them in various poses, some quite erotic, with a deft flick of his stick.

You are amazing, I told him. He smiled, more to himself than at me. *I have been drawing all of my life. It's how I think. Some people express their thoughts with words, others through music, still others keep their thoughts to themselves.*

We watched the sunset and the moonrise, hardly speaking, simply nodding and smiling at each other, even laughing aloud when he created an especially interesting character. He knew the villa I was renting and told me that Ernest Hemingway had rented it years ago. He invited me stay at his villa for the night. I accepted.

We ate like kings and drank sangria as we spoke of art, love, war, politics, eroticism, and other important topics. He would occasionally test my limited Spanish. *Como se llamo? Alan. Y usted? Yo Pablo.*

I awoke to Mozart's Grand Partita. Pablo was on his veranda, and I joined him there to enjoy the sunrise. After breakfast we walked to the beach. Pablo carried his stick. I carried a basket of wine, bread, and leftover grilled shrimp.

We resumed our discourse, laughing, crying and shouting at each other. Pablo expressed his rare insight into life with wit, charm, anger, love, and great fervor. Finally he said: *Amigo, I would like to give you a gift, to remind you of our time together and reveal the relationship that has formed between us.*

He began to draw in the sand with his stick, creating hilarious and provocative scenes between two people, recognizable as Pablo and I. His stick was a magic wand. I told him I was amazed at how little planning seemed to go into each scene. He told me that if he knew how a drawing was going to turn out, why bother to draw it. And isn't that true about life?

The scenes became complete pictures that grew into a mural in the sand, four or five feet high, and at least twelve feet wide. A masterpiece. *I will dedicate it to you if you agree to stay tonight.* I agreed, and he wrote: "Por me amigo, Alan. Picasso 1968"

We retreated to his veranda. As the sun drifted lower, the drawing became a painting, a gouache with ever-changing colors. The figures leaped from the sand, dancing, frolicking. And then a horrible thought struck me. As the tide came in, I would lose my masterpiece.

At first the water drifted over the images and quickly retreated, revealing ever deepening grooves, much like an acid bath does to the etching plate. Gradually, the figures elongated into Modigliani-like figures. My masterpiece gradually became a blur, and eventually, the water receded to reveal the blank smoothness of the sand.

Oh well, I sighed, *easy come easy go.* Picasso disagreed. *You contributed to our escapade because your life—your victories, defeats, won and lost loves, joys—has created its own masterpiece—YOU, Alan—and at great cost. So the drawing was not easy come. You invested your life in it. I know, too, that it is indelibly imprinted in your mind's eye, to see whenever you choose. It is a gift for you alone, amigo. For my gifts to the world I charge a great deal of money.*

Picasso recognized what his fame had earned him. During the last dozen years of his life, he paid for everything by check.

People knew that his signature was far more valuable than the amount of the checks, so when he died, the amount of uncashed checks was in the millions of dollars.

Viva Picasso! And thank you, amigo. I still enjoy my painting.

Hello, Dali!

W hen I lived on the East Coast, I visited New York for my art, theater and food fix. One afternoon, I was enjoying High Tea at the St. Regis hotel, a stomping ground for Salvador Dali, or *Maestro*, as he preferred to be called. Sure enough, this day The Maestro was seated several tables away, surrounded by his usual entourage, holding court in his inimitable style.

Dali was more than an artist. He was a work of art. Dali was the darling of the media, but he used the press as much as they used him. For example, at a press conference in Washington, D. C., after one of his paintings had been hung in the National Gallery of Art, a reporter asked, "Maestro, where do you get your inspiration?" Without hesitation, Dali replied, "From my left testicle." The next day, *The Washington Post* reported that Salvador Dali had once again displayed bizarre behavior, complete with a close up of the Maestro.

His appearance contributed to his image, from his one-of-a-kind moustache and shoulder length hair to his attire. This day he wore a ruffled white lace shirt with diamond pin and a black cape with white lining draped around his shoulders. He held a black lacquer walking stick with an enormous carved silver handle. As he sipped tea, his pinky aimed skyward displaying an ornate ring the size of a walnut.

A man approached Dali's table and asked: *"Mr. Dali, may I have your autograph, please?"* He was not prepared for what followed.

"I am not 'mister.' I am The Maestro. The cost of interrupting my tea and obtaining my autograph is fifty dollars. Cash." With that, Dali set down his cup and put out his hand— palm up. The man looked over his shoulder at his wife. She nodded and he laid three twenties in Dali's palm. Dali put them on the table, pulled a pen from his shirt pocket, and signed the napkin in front of him. Realizing Dali was not about to give him

change, the man left, mumbling a thank you. Dali beckoned to the waiter and gave him the three twenties.

Stories about Dali's behavior circulated throughout the hotel via the underground communication system [the help]. This is my favorite:

A High Society Hostess lived in a penthouse suite atop the St. Regis. She pulled off quite a coup when Dali agreed to be her guest of honor at a dinner party. Rumor has it that he required six months' advance notice.

My report of the event is based on information provided by hotel employees. According to the doorman, "It looked like a parade of Rolls Royces the evening of the event." Earlier in the day, a bevy of exotic flowers were delivered, including rare orchids imported to decorate the dining room table. The hotel manager insisted that the caterer had never created such an extravagant feast. The dining room table was set for twenty-six, with several smaller "satellite" tables for second tier guests.

A further account comes from hotel staffers present. The party was a smashing success. Dali reveled in the limelight, entertaining guests with his usual flamboyance and charm. No one could work a crowd like him. FDR, JFK and LBJ, known for their ability to charm your socks off, were amateurs compared with The Maestro. He was charming, while he commanded respect, even awe. Moments after the last guest left, Dali heard sobbing. He found the distraught Madame X in the dining room, crying loudly, tears streaming down her face.

What is your problem, Madame? Your party was a great success. She pointed to a hole in a corner of the lace tablecloth. *It's ruined. It was made especially for tonight. It took six months, and now it's ruined.*

Dali spread the tablecloth smoothly on the table and pulled a pen from his pocket. He drew a face, using the hole as an eye. Not stopping there, using the entire tablecloth, he drew the body of a woman reclining on a sofa.

Voila! The tablecloth could not have cost more than thirty thousand dollars. Now, he exclaimed, as he signed his name with flair, *you have a masterpiece by the Maestro Himself worth five times that!*

Potpourri and the Top Ten

I was watching the Classic Arts Channel the other night, and a group was playing a Schubert String Quartet. As recent as twenty years ago I would have found the piece boring. It struck me that my taste in music had grown to a higher level.

But what about the people who grew up listening to opera, only to later hear and appreciate jazz, pop, rock and roll, country. My son, Richard, went the other way. He grew up on rock and roll and loves, equally well, jazz and classical music. It seems your tastes can grow in either direction.

Kenneth Clarke, in his award winning series on Civilization, concluded that Michelangelo's *David* represented a higher level of civilization than a two thousand-year old African mask. If that's true, then whatever has come after Michelangelo would represent an upward progression. Sorry, Sir Kenneth, but I do not think that today's neon art, exciting as it is, beats *David* any more than Andy Warhol's *Campbell's Soup* is at a higher level than DaVinci's *Last Supper.*

* * * * *

A Federal Court issued an order that funds withheld from the Brooklyn Museum be released to the museum. You will recall that New York Mayor Giuliani wanted the funds withheld because he found the art in an African exhibit offensive. For more on the issue, read my last column. You do save them, don't you?

* * * * *

A word about buying art on the Internet: CAUTION! I recently scrolled through a litany of "works of art" by such notable names as Picasso, Chagall and Miro. The works were described as *lithographs, prints, originals,* and a few other equally invalid euphemisms.

I called about two Picasso's listed as hand signed original etchings. The owner of the pieces assured me they were valid, even though they were not listed in the Bloch catalog, which contains every Picasso graphic. He also said he had just acquired a catalogued piece, also hand signed, which he would gladly sell me. I looked up the piece in my catalog and found that the edition was unsigned. I didn't bother to call him back to ask him who signed it.

Lithograph may be the most misleading term of them all. It could mean anything from an original work of art to a worthless reproduction. Artists create lithographs by drawing directly onto limestone blocks. There is generally a separate block for each color. After the edition of works has been pulled, the blocks are destroyed. The examples printed from those blocks are original lithographs. On the other hand, the cover of *TIME* is an offset lithograph, made from photo negatives. It is a reproduction, which can be produced in the hundreds, thousands or millions. The Chagall and Miro pieces offered were reproductions, worth $20-50. Bidding started at over a hundred dollars, and two were in the $500 range. Ditto for a suite of reproductions by Francisco Zuniga.

* * * * *

As the year comes to a close, it is time for a list of the ten most important artists of the 20th century, selected by you. Not an easy task. The 20th Century produced an unrivaled range of styles in art. Clearly the criteria used to assess aesthetic and technical aspects of art have to be re-examined as to their relevancy and adequacy. Some measures are obsolete; and with the ever-growing use of new media and technology, different standards need to be developed. World wars, many other skirmishes, political upheaval and an ever-shrinking planet have all had significant impact on the arts, which reflect and anticipate reality. The range of 20th Century art includes representational, abstract art, cubism, surrealism, the last of impressionism, DaDa, German Expressionism, Fauvism, Abstract Impressionism, and Pop Art--to name some of the more influential schools.

Thanks to readers who sent me their top ten lists. Here are the results:

Pablo Picasso appeared at the top of ninety-five percent of the lists, and was never listed lower than second. Next was Henri Matisse, followed closely by Joan Miro and Claude Monet. Fifth on the list: Salvador Dali, who edged out Marc Chagall. In the seventh spot came sculptor Auguste Rodin. The father of non-objective art, Wassily Kandinsky garnered the eighth spot [He was second to Picasso on my list]. The top ten list was rounded out by two Americans, namely, Andy Warhol and Alexander Calder [another sculptor, and father of the mobile].

Only Dali [1904] and Warhol [1928] were born in this century; and only Rodin [1917], Monet [1926] and Matisse [1954] died before 1973. Clearly, there was ample opportunity for artists born in this century to make their mark--and most of them didn't. Only two women, both American, received any votes, Georgia O'Keefe and Mary Cassatt. Other important vote getters included Jackson Pollock, Henry Moore, Pierre Renoir, Georges Braque, Paul Klee, Fernand Leger, and Giorgio de Chirico. No votes for Magritte, Man Ray, Rivera, or de Kooning.

So where are we, and where are we headed, as we enter the 21st century? In a world of rapidly evolving technology and a global explosion of human rights and freedom of expression, the future is limitless. We already have digital photography, neon, and videos, so it is likely that by the end of the next century, there will be art genres and forms of expression we cannot yet imagine.

* * * * *

Make a New Year's resolution to visit three museum exhibits in 2000, including at least one featuring art you neither appreciate nor understand. And take a teenager with you.

Music to My Eyes

I was in the middle of hanging paintings that Ivan Dobroruka
had sent to me for his one-man show at my gallery, when Ivan
came in and told me he had just finished the last one. I climbed
down the ladder to behold a beautiful watercolor and crayon
drawing of the inside of a cathedral, complete with organ, altar
and stained glass windows. Ivan asked me to give it a name, since
he invariably agreed with my titles of his works.

I closed my eyes and the lyrical quality of the piece quickly
became apparent. I could hear the organ playing! I recognized the
melody. Bach! Definitely Bach! *I can hear it,* I exclaimed. *It's a
toccata by Bach. Let's call it "Toccata by Bach."* Ivan smiled
and replied, *Very good, Alan, but which toccata is it?* I smiled
back. Few musical works are as famous as Toccata and Fugue in
D Minor, with its intense rhythmic and driving force, elaborate
atmosphere and astonishing echo effects obtained by changing
keyboards. Ivan had captured its essence, its joyous and dynamic
theme, in his drawing. I practically shouted it to him. And that's
what we called it.

There is an undeniable relationship among all the arts.
Dobroruka also created four etchings, depicting sonnets by
Shakespeare. Each captures the essence of the sonnet it
represents. Illustrations are an integral part of children's books,
translating words into pictures. The integration of music into the
movies adds to the emotional, even visual impact of scenes. We
are more familiar with the notion of adding music to visual art.
Going the other way is less prevalent. It is a more abstract
extrapolation. However, I cannot listen to Beethoven's 6th
symphony, without seeing fields of flowers, trees and meadows.
The melodies and rhythms of the Pastoral Symphony create visual
illusions of spring.

How about the imagery conjured up by Rossini's William Tell
Overture? Can anyone familiar with the Lone Ranger hear the

opening strains of that Overture and not picture the Masked Man aboard his trusty stallion, Silver, riding into the sunset amidst cries of, *Hi ho, Silver, Away.*

The relationship between the arts is logical. It is why artists branch into different art forms. Their creativity is not bound by one area of expertise or success. Anthony Quinn and Tony Bennett are not just an actor and a singer who paint for a hobby. They are serious artists, as was Red Skeleton and a host of other actors and musicians. Many songwriters write music and lyrics, and actors have become directors, which requires more than the ability to interpret scripts and characters. They must be adept at visual interpretations, as well. There are the Steve Martins, Woody Allens and Anthony Newleys of the world. They do it all: write it, direct it and act in it. Newley wrote musicals, so he also wrote the music--and sang it. Still, to see what a fugue played on an organ looks like, is some kind of a miracle. Pure magic.

During the Renaissance Age, art showed angels with wings and halos on Mary and Jesus. Since those notions were mainstream thought, the imagery was not considered unreal, although I have always thought of that art as the forerunner of surrealism. The surrealists, from de Chirico to Matta [the last living surrealist at 90], stressed the subconscious and used hallucination and the fantastic to arrive at reality through non-real imagery. Salvador Dali's melting clocks exemplify non-real imagery.

Another artist, Carol Kucera, took the magic to another height. She was chosen by NASA to chronicle Sally Ride's ride. Other artists painted the rocket, the launch, portraits of the astronauts, their families, officials and other onlookers. Not Carol. She painted Sally's thoughts and emotions. A nouveau abstract expressionist, Carol gave spontaneous expression to the unconscious. NASA's museum curator was skeptical about using her work. In the end, his decision to include the piece, and feature it as the centerfold in the book that accompanied a world tour of the art, proved more than correct. Throughout the United States and abroad, it was the most talked about work. The colors, shapes, and rhythms in Carol's abstract work captured Sally

Ride's feelings: She is excited and filled with anticipation, fear and joy. Kucera also wrote a poem while watching the launch, and that is also on display at the NASA museum.

The next time you look at a work of art, look for a hidden meaning, an emotion the artist is attempting to depict or evoke from you. I find that kind of art the most interesting. It's like music to my eyes!

Can You See What You Hear?

W hen my friend, Lori Barth, invited me to the opening of a show by her husband, I said *Yes* immediately. Familiar with Bob Leatherbarrow's artistry, I knew it would be a thoroughly satisfying evening. It exceeded my expectations.

I liked all eleven pieces. They spanned a wide range of creativity and spontaneity, unified with similar strokes and technique. Each was completely different. Some were playful with bright colors and a spirited energy. Lots of blank space yet amazingly tight with unmistakable underlying rhythm. Others were subdued, subtle in soft, pastel shades, A few were almost dark. All were expressive and dynamic, with rich textures and complex interplays.

Bumpin in the Basement, the signature work of the show, was a crowd favorite. It is colorful, with exciting tones, and dramatic shades and rhythms. Abstract, it is surprisingly easy to follow, held together by Bob's deft use of underlying themes and a familiar yet fresh rhythm. *Rush Hour*, is more abstract, with separate themes magically held together by a driving beat. I could definitely feel the frenetic nature of rush hour in LA. Another favorite is *Don't Mess with the Messenger*, a work of charming interplay and humor. None is more beautiful than *Willows*. The soft pastel tones, rich layering and soft counter themes made me feel fuzzy all over. This is a masterpiece, a poem without words, suggesting non-objective yet clearly identifiable pastoral images.

Now for the good news: you can own all of these wonderful works and enjoy them in your own home at your convenience. Or in your car, at the beach, wherever. Bob Leatherbarrow is a jazz drummer, and he introduced his newest album, *Bumpin in the Basement*, at one of LA's top jazz clubs last month. This CD could put Bob at the next level in his burgeoning career. It hit the charts in terms of airplay on jazz stations across the country almost immediately and has been climbing ever since. If you like good music, check it out. The label is *Chartmaker Jazz*. The other players in his quartet are also talented and successful in their own right: Mitchel Forman on piano, Reggie Hamilton on bass, and Ernie Watts on tenor saxophone join Bob in a celebration of music.

I kept you in the dark about Bob's art form to show how similar terms describe different art mediums. And the relationship between visual art and music is strong. Little wonder that so many musicians draw or paint.

* * * * * * * *

Don't miss *Van Gogh's Van Goghs: Masterpieces from the Van Gogh Museum, Amsterdam* at the LA County Museum of Art. The exhibit closes on May 16. What a success for LACMA! Over 250,000 people have visited the show, and over half a million tickets have been sold. A score for LA art lovers. The show was on display in the Fall of 1998 at the National Gallery of Art in Washington, D. C. It was the most attended art exhibit in the world last year. As a matter of fact, the top five attended exhibits world-wide in 1998 were all in the United States. Evidently we have more art lovers than we get credit for from the rest of the world.

Don't wait for the blockbuster shows that come through our museums. LACMA has an outstanding and varied permanent collection. Check it out with your kids. Exposure to art improves the appreciation of it. With the demise of the National Endowment of the Arts and the low priority the arts get in schools, our children are not being exposed to art, which is definitive evaluation of a society.

I enjoyed *Old Masters Prints from the LACMA Collection from the Fifteenth to the Seventeenth Century* [ends May 31]. Albrecht Durer and Rembrandt van Rijn head up an all-star cast. Durer's engravings and woodcuts have yet to be improved upon, and Rembrandt remains unsurpassed as an etcher.

Works of art on paper are not often displayed, because they are fragile and sensitive to light. They also get overlooked in our "BIGGER & LOUDER" Society. An intricate etching is a string quartet, in contrast with a symphony played by a hundred musicians. Or someone whispering *I love you* in your ear instead of over a loudspeaker. Thanks to Victor Carlson, senior curator of prints and drawings at the Los Angeles County Museum, who organized the exhibit.

Infinity in Finite Form

I magine a menorah in sterling silver with Stars of David adorning the individual candleholders. Now imagine those candleholders spinning like dreidles. Add moving arms of the menorah, rotating slowly in opposite directions, creating the illusion of a labyrinth. Can you see it, flickering flames celebrating the miracle of Chanukah, surrounded by Judaism in motion?

Yaacov Agam envisioned it twenty years ago. Then he created it, and it was a centerpiece of the one-man show I held for him, in which he clearly established, through his art, his importance as a twentieth century master and a spokesman for Art and Judaism. As various pieces arrived at my gallery prior to the show, I was struck as much by the scope of techniques and art forms, as I was by the aesthetic beauty of the individual pieces. From polymorphic paintings [3-D works that change as your view of them changes] to tapestries; from serigraphs to Agamographs [overlaid lithographs that provide, in a different way, polymorphic views]; from transformable sculptures to colorful cubes which became chairs at the touch of a spring-loaded button, and were used at a dinner party commemorating the opening of the Agam retrospective at the Guggenheim Museum in New York.

Our society refers to advancing creativity as *pushing the envelope.* Agam goes farther. His art leaps boundaries, leaving previous limits in the distant past. His art is a spaceship compared to the horse drawn carriage of the recent past. It is the computer to pen and ink. It is boundless, beyond the imagination of mere mortals. He lives the same way. He once told me that, when he knew he could swim three miles, he would swim out two miles so his survival depended on him swimming four miles to make it back. When we were about to tape an interview for television, he noticed some notes I had scribbled on an index card that I stuck in a book he wrote. Ten seconds before airtime, he grabbed the book from me and threw it offstage.

What makes Agam tick is rooted in Judaism. His art, which at first glance appears to be colorful geometric patterns and clever metal structures, is steeped in Judaic symbolism and Law. Art & Reality is an underlying theme in his art, along with the Second Commandment, which forbids graven images. His art is a much a quest and a concept as it is a visual representation.

Agam points out that Abraham proclaimed a unique attribute of God for the first time—an *invisible* God. In no other religion is God so totally invisible. Buddhism, Christianity, even Islam that opposes all images, proclaim an earthly incarnation of God. Just as God is invisible in Judaism, in life the essence of power is invisible. The reality or force behind any action is hidden from the eye.

He views the biblical use of a rainbow as the first example of art that reflects the essence of reality. Its underlying essence is invisible light which, when broken a certain way, yields its beautiful colors. We see the consequence of the action of light, but the full essence behind the rainbow—light itself—is not visible. In his work, Agam tries to capture this same invisible, endless reality behind things.

In most of his works, when you can see the right side, you don't see the left side; you can't see their beginning and end within clearly marked boundaries. They are always transformable, with almost infinite ways of seeing them. In this way, his art reflects the power and uniqueness inherent in the most meaningful reality of existence—the invisible forces behind everything.

Thus his art demonstrates the principle of reality as a continuous "becoming" rather than a circumscribed statement. And Agam has been deeply influenced by the Judaism conception that reality cannot be represented in a graven image, and that what is seen consists of fragmented images that can never be grasped as a whole. This led Agam to create images, which could not be seen completely at any one time. Such images make the viewer conscious of the idea that he is receiving partial revelation behind which lie unseen levels of reality.

Perpetual coming into being. The new face[s] of art. That is the legacy of Yaacov Agam.

A Star is Reborn

A dear friend of mine received horrific news. He needed surgery to remove a tumor. Probably malignant. Then the doctors found more stuff, which had to be removed. Also life-threatening. So why am I burdening you with the problems of my friend? After all, I can deal with the adversities of life as they occur, to my friends or me. But there is a story behind the story.

When I last spoke to my friend, he exuded an optimism that bodes well for him. He is facing life with higher expectations than he has in years, and he has always been very healthy. He is hearing music in his dreams and remembering what he hears. That might not seem important to you, and wouldn't be to me if I were in his situation and dreaming tunes. But my friend is a composer, a musician of the first order, with a career that spans nearly three decades, with dozens of albums and CD's on his own, with various groups he put together. Although he is not a household name, he has a solid reputation and following here and across the Pond.

Only a scant percentage of musicians have lasted from the '70's to the present, and only a handful of those have consistently produced winners. Tastes in music change, the dominant buying group of pop music is early to mid-teens, so you can count on your fingers the artists who were popular thirty years ago and are still popular. They run out of ideas and create nothing, or they continue to compose the kind of music they succeeded with way back when. Only when isn't now, so the struggle is constant, to produce what sells, without selling yourself out.

That has been my friend's dilemma for the twelve years I have known him. He has enjoyed successes, but his refusal to compromise his artistic vision has often made his life challenging. Things have suddenly and irrevocably changed. He is facing the greatest challenge of his life.

Funny how that works. In the nineteenth century, after

contracting tuberculosis before he was twenty, Franz Schubert wrote the most beautiful music of his short-lived career. Before he passed on at the age of 31, he composed his magnificent 8th ["Unfinished"] Symphony, as well as "Serenade" and "Ave Maria," generally regarded as among the most beautiful melodies ever penned. The melodies came to Schubert in dreams and while awake, walking down the street. He would frantically write the notes on his sleeve, so he wouldn't forget what he was hearing. Ludwig von Beethoven wrote the quintessential piece of music, his 9th Symphony ["Ode to Joy"], and other masterpieces, after he was completely deaf. Little doubt that Beethoven heard the music that he wrote down. I believe that he heard the music in its purist form, in his mind's eye, or mind's ear, if you prefer, free of any man-made noise or distractions. As though God whispered it to him.

Perhaps God is whispering some of his favorite tunes to my friend. Just the other day, he told Patty and me that he was hearing music from heaven in dreams. Write it down, mate. From God's lips to your ears, to the public. I have no doubt that it will be a time of rejuvenation, a victory for the inner spirit, as my friend offers us the music of his soul.

Some of the greatest art has been born in the clutches of personal angst and agony. Besides Schubert and Beethoven, there is John Milton, who was blind when he dictated his epic masterpiece, "Paradise Lost." Toulouse Lautrec, Vincent van Gogh and Auguste Renoir painted timeless masterpieces in the throws of despair and physical pain.

For some artists, personal and commercial successes occur simultaneously. No depression. No deprivation required. But there is certain magic to the art of those who suffer. That suffering touches their soul, and enables them to reach artistic levels that might otherwise not be accessible. The trick, it seems, is for them to accept the suffering, remove the self-pity, and recognize the opportunity to achieve greatness.

We can all learn a lesson from him.

On January 22, 2002 my dear friend, Pete Bardens finally succumbed to cancer and passed away, his daughter, Tallulah, and son, Sam, at his side. His latest endeavor, "The Art of Levitation," with pal Mick Fleetwood on drums and Tallulah on vocals, will be released posthumously. You will be missed, Pete, but you and your music will live in my heart forever.

Genius Doesn't Know Celebrity

H ow does one decide who is a good artist and who isn't? Shakespeare would say that the question is based on an erroneous assumption. In the words of Hamlet: "Things are neither good nor bad but thinking makes them so." Unfortunately, we live in a society where we rank everything. First is best. And nobody remembers second.

My home page on the Internet consistently solicits my vote for best LA restaurant, best burger, best coffee, best burrito, best view, best this, best that. We give awards for Best Actor, Best Song, Best Movie, and the rest. It would be more accurate to substitute the word *favorite* for the word *best*. Popularity is the primary criterion for determining who is best at anything.

That creates a problem. Vincent Van Gogh never sold a painting during his lifetime. I don't count the one his brother, an art dealer, bought for a client, who decided not to buy it. Edgar Degas never sold a piece to a museum while he was alive. And the critics and curators looked down on Toulouse Lautrec during his short life. Similar examples abound in literature and music. Walt Whitman had to publish his poetry, because no one else would.

I bring this up because Patty and I recently went to an open house at the showroom of an art dealer friend of mine. He has been a major supplier of fine art to galleries throughout the United States for over thirty years. He has a great eye and excellent taste in art, theater, music, food, wine, and most of the other things that interest me. I have known Basil for over twenty years and am familiar with his inventory, so I went to the open house as a show of support and for the excellent champagne, rather that with the idea of discovering something new.

Scattered through the six or seven rooms were large and colorful works by an artist I did not know. Her name is *Janek* [pronounced "Janeek"]. Contemporary, filled with energy and color, some pieces were reminiscent of Miro, others of Picasso, with a little Matisse and the Abstract Expressionists thrown in for flavor. She is not derivative of any of them--more of a synthesis of them into a style distinctively her own.

She is a "local" artist, living and teaching right here in Southern California, transplanted from Armenia. Basil introduced us, and her demeanor immediately struck me. She is friendly, with a hearty handshake and laugh, seemingly uninhibited, and, as Patty and I spent time with her, more and more playful and soulful. Her art is unabashedly an extension of her personality. I had never seen her work in my twenty-eight years as an art dealer, although her talent is unmistakable, her art a treat to behold.

The previous Friday night, Patty and I went to a concert in honor of one my dearest and closest friends, Peter Bardens. A transplant from England, Pete is a musician—a brilliant composer and keyboard player. He has enormous talent, has sold millions of albums and CD's, and has played with household names. His own group, *CAMEL*, toured America in the seventies and played at the prestigious Prince Albert Hall in London. Over twenty years since they were together, *Deutsche Gramophone* released a 2-CD set of the best of Camel.

Among the artists who came to honor and play with Pete was Mick Fleetwood [who was in a band with Pete in England nearly forty years ago], Sheila E., who played with Prince, Joe Walsh from the Eagles, saxophonist Don Caz, John Mayall, and other talented performers, including Pete's daughter, Tallulah. Pete's stature and reputation among his peers far exceeds his public recognition, although he did make Downbeat's top 20 list of rock and roll keyboard players of all time. Still, it would not surprise me if you have not heard of him.

Janek and Peter Bardens represent the unknown talent in the arts. They do art for art's sake, and those who are touched by their creations are blessed. Too bad for the rest of the world. It is *their* loss.

I am dismayed that some of the most talented artists often toil in relative obscurity. I mentioned my feelings to Patty as we were driving home from Basil's place. She smiled and put it in proper perspective:

"GENIUS DOESN'T KNOW CELEBRITY!"

They Also Serve

P atty's sister, Marge, knows that we enjoy going to the theater. Whenever we visit Minneapolis [that's where Patty's family lives], we make sure we go at least one night. Last year we saw a highly entertaining Stephen Sondheim production at the Guthrie Lab. There are lots of terrific local theater groups in Minneapolis, perhaps the most per capita in the country. Marge sent us a comprehensive list of everything playing during our last visit.

We picked a play by an ensemble group in the suburbs and told Marge to get us tickets. She took it to another level, and nine of us went to see the show, compliments of Millie, the family matriarch. We saw *I Love you, You're Perfect, Now Change*. It was hilarious, poignant, beautifully staged, cleverly produced, fast-paced, and brilliantly performed by four actors who played a few dozen parts between them. Driving back to the hotel after the performance, Patty and I marveled at the quality of the event.

We especially enjoyed and admired the actors. Their talent was matched by their enthusiasm and the passion they brought to their work. One actor has been a member of the troupe for twenty years and teaches and performs at a local improv company. He and the other three are actors, plain and simple. They are doing what they love, not for fame or fortune, but for the sheer joy of acting. They represent hundreds, even thousands of actors across the country, who are glad to perform for meager wages.

Just because they toil in anonymity, do not for a moment think that they are therefore devoid of talent. Au contraire. Fame and fortune are accidents. Dedicated actors may not have either thrust upon them. But they may have as much talent as others who are struck with the F & F lightning bolt. As host James Lipton noted on "Inside the Actor's Studio," there were seven years between welfare and Whoopie Goldberg's Academy Award nomination for Best Actress in *The Color Purple*.

The thing about being an artist is, that's what you are, whatever the art form. It doesn't matter what kind of artist: actor, playwright, musician, screenwriter, painter, whatever. Even if you are waiting tables, serving drinks, sweeping trash, driving a cab, an artist is an artist. Those are the jobs that artists do while pursuing their dreams. I know a number of artists who teach privately or in schools, because they cannot sell enough works to support themselves. And a few are in numerous museums.

Since so few people really love what they do, but are "stuck" in lousy job situations because they pay is good or the bills are high, it is hard to imagine that others would do it for low pay. The artist doesn't care. Anything to enable them to pursue their addiction. Carol Kucera, a very talented artist I represented in the late 1970's to mid-80's, once told me that I was lucky. I could get out of the art business any time I wanted and pursue another profession. She was stuck. She was an artist. It was in her blood. And she was right. Fortunately, Carol is alive and well and successful, now selling her art out of Sante Fe, New Mexico and on the internet.

I can relate to artists, because I am a fringe artist. That's what a columnist is. Oh, I had a book published about a dozen years ago, which still sells on the internet and in a few bookstores. A handful of short stories have appeared in print. Several other books never got that far. Ditto for a play and a couple of screenplay treatments. I have also appeared in a movie and a few commercials. Basically, though, I tried the writer's route for a few years, but I always had the luxury of being an art dealer at the same time. For me, it is better than serving food and drinks. I already did that a number of years ago, when I owned a nightclub.

The point is, the next time you get served a martini and the bartender says she is a singer or an actor, recognize that she is telling the truth. And she represents those talented people who provide joy to the rest of us. She is simply waiting her turn.

Hawkeye Understands
J. S. Bach

O ne of my favorite M*A*S*H episodes revolved around Radar O'Reilly's pursuit of a visiting nurse who loved classical music. Hawkeye and B. J. were constantly advising the naive corporal as to how to woo the lovely lady. One day, Radar asked them what to say when the nurse asked him what he though of Bach. Hawkeye's replied: "Roll yours eyes upward, purse your lips, nod, and simply say: 'Ahh! Bach!'" And it worked!

Last night, the Los Angeles Opera put on a performance of Bach's *Requiem Mass in B Minor*, a two-hour masterpiece with no intermission. You could have heard a pin drop at the Dorothy Chandler. I mean, no one coughed. No one moved. It seemed as though no one breathed, that we held our collective breath.

I collect requiem masses, my favorites being Mozart, Verdi and Berlioz. All three are filled with exquisite melodies and dramatic passages with volume, contrast and intensity. Passion in your face. I often feel my blood race as I am drawn into the solitude of death and redemption. I was not sure that Bach could do that for me.

He didn't. Not at first. The chorus started in a low-keyed manner, with typical Bach syncopation with the orchestra. Interesting rhythms interspersed with mathematical precision. My finger gently tapped involuntarily against my knee in concert with the beat. A while later, I noticed that my entire hand was moving with the beat as though I were conducting the orchestra and chorus, and my foot was tapping. I also realized that I hand no feeling in the rest of my body. I was numb. It was asleep. Not just like when you go to bed. More like when you cross your leg for a long time and when you uncross it, your foot is asleep, fuzzy, no feeling in it, except the pins and needles who you do move it.

I had become completely absorbed by the music. Unlike Mozart and friends, I was not overtly overwhelmed by the music. The music was in me. I was subtly drawn into the deepest part of my subconscious. My mind was racing. My heart was racing. Imagery of different shapes and colors passed before my closed eyes. Ideas for personal renewal sprang into my head. I struggled with my own sense of existence. I questioned my purpose. I thanked the Almighty for my life and asked for greater understanding of it. Without a lot of noise, without rancor, without in-your-face volume and passion, Bach had woven his web in my heart and head. Finally, the last line of the Mass came into focus: *Grant me peace.* He—God—did that, through his agent, Johan Sebastian Bach and the miracle of his music.

I have not been that moved by a work of art since I stood before *La Pieta* in the Vatican, in awe of its beauty and translucence, mesmerized by its authentic spiritual power. Ironically, these two works of art are Catholic symbols, which perform their miracle on the son of an orthodox Jew [I am far less religious than my father].

Another interesting perspective is that these great works of art are different mediums--music and sculpture. Art for the ears and art for the eyes. The greatest Artist, the Almighty, out of which all creativity springs, creates art that fills all our senses. Whether He is sweeping his brush across the horizon offering a spectacular sunset on the ocean or filling a meadow with waves of flowers offering fragrances as beautiful and heady and their shapes and colors, we are swept into the world of art. Likewise, there is beauty to the touch and to the taste.

What all art has in common is that it is for the Soul. If you have not found art that nourishes your soul, you are missing out on the beauty of art. Worse: you are missing the beauty of life. Perhaps you are too busy caught up in the hunt to enjoy the woods in which the hunt is taking place. Catching the fox has its thrill, but it is short-lived. Art endures. Get out there and find it. You'll be glad you did.

Peace of Mind is in the Notes

*F*ifty years ago, I was on my way home from school in the midst of a severe snowstorm. For a Southern city, Washington gets its share of snow. And this was late March. My 1949 Studebaker's windshield wipers moved at one speed, bumpy, and the defroster had one level, low and intermittent. To keep my nerves from jangling, I listened to Paul Hume's Classical Hour on WOL 1450AM. I joined in, humming along to a Mozart ditty from *Eine Kleine Nacht Musik*. I smiled all the way home, and laughed aloud when Paul announced that some critics considered the piece "immature." He went on to announce that Wolfgang was nine when he wrote it.

I mention this in light of a column that Michael Kimmelman recently wrote for the New York Times, lamenting the fade-out of classical radio. Michael cited several disturbing events. First, New York's classical station, WNYC-FM93.9, cut five hours of music from its broadcast. Second, National Public Radio [NPR] gutted *Performance Today*, its classical music show, replacing it with talk radio.

Private stations featuring classical music have been disappearing for years. I recently learned, while listening to my favorite station, KUSC Public Radio [91.5FM] in Los Angeles, that such cities as Miami and Philadelphia had lost their classical stations. Philadelphia? Home of one of the greatest symphony orchestras in the world!

There are so few classical stations left, if they had names like "kimono dragon" or "giant condor," they would be on the endangered species list. And there is no one fighting for their survival.

I understand that it is good business to replace classical music with more profitable pop programming. I admit that I treated my art galleries as a business, not a museum. Although I provided a public service of sorts, by presenting and promoting fine art, making a living was my *raison d'etre*. A newspaper critic once complained that I was more interested in selling art than simply showing it for the public's pleasure and edification. I agreed with her and promised to change my attitude when the Washington Post stopped accepting advertising.

But NPR and other nonprofit stations are not supposed to be about money. Theirs is a different, higher purpose. Or so I thought. When President Lyndon Johnson signed the Public Radio Act near the end of his administration, he declared: *With all the goods and services we produce, we want most of all to enrich man's spirit.*

Growing up, I actually had classical music choices. In addition to the nightly Paul Hume Show, there was WGMS, a twenty-four classical music station serving the Washington, D. C. Area. I learned to appreciate classical music at a young age. Radio station owners and managers may want to revisit the commercial pros and cons of classical radio. I advertised events at my galleries in the Washington Post, WMAL Radio [the #1 listened to station in the area], and WGMS, which had a small fraction of the listening audience, thus costing me the least. Guess where I got the greatest response. Apparently people who enjoy classical music enjoy all the arts, as well as other fine things. Regular advertisers included top restaurants, luxury automobile dealerships, the finest jewelry stores--you get the picture.

Perhaps the trend toward talk radio reflects our need to exercise free speech. Listeners talk back from the safety of their cars. Have you noticed those people at stop lights? They are in heated arguments. With whom? For some, it is a way to yell at their mate or their boss without getting interrupted. Others are simply venting.

Given the opportunity to listen, or perhaps being forced to listen to classical music, people might find great music soothing, relaxing. People in the medical profession have recognized the value of art therapy. For example, the UCLA cardiac Rehabilitation Center offers lectures on the benefits of art in therapy and rehabilitation.

There is a poignant scene in the movie, *Children of a Lesser God*, when William Hurt comes home after a tough day and immediately puts on J. S. Bach's *Double Violin Concerto*. His deaf girlfriend, Marilee Matlee, asks him to describe what the music sounds like and how it affects him. Hurt's facial and body expressions pour out his emotions and demonstrate the concerto's beauty and affect on him. He expresses complete surrender and tranquility, and, as the scene ends, Matlee, too, is caught up in the music. THAT is what great art can do. As an announcer recently said on KUSC [NPR in Los Angeles]: *Music is not to be seen, or just heard. Music is for the heart—from the heart.*

If you have a station like KUSC in your area, give it a try. If not, buy a CD or two of classical music. Listen during drive time, when the traffic is especially annoying and you are losing your patience. Give it a chance. A week or more. If that doesn't convince you, buy two more and allow a month.

I promise that it will eventually click in, and when the right music and moment coincide, your life will be changed for the better, and forever.

No Strings Attached

*T*hose of you who read this column, even on an occasional basis, will be pleased with my latest revelation: there might be hope for the arts, after all!

Don't get too excited. The arts still receive second-class status in the allocation of Government funds, at the Federal, State and local levels. And they still are largely dismissed in our schools' priorities, behind athletics of all sorts. Interest groups still fight for the right of girls to play organized soccer, softball, basketball, and track [can football and wrestling be far behind], while no one fights for the right of any student to learn a musical instrument, take dancing, drama, or engage in other aesthetic or cultural pursuits. Do we really believe that there is more to be learned from softball than an appreciation, through exposure, to Shakespeare, Tchaikovsky and Michelangelo? Rest assured I will stay firmly planted on my soapbox and bemoan the dearth of art appreciation by our politicians and educators.

So why my optimisim? What has caused me to hold out hope? It is based, I must reveal, on a very unscientific survey. A survey of two children. Two little girls, both of whom are very special. Their names are Kate and Anna. They recently turned seven years old, Kate on July 27th, Anna on August 2nd. Talking to their parents revealed what they wanted most for their birthdays. You will never guess.

Katie, who had just completed a summer mini-camp for painting and ceramics, and in the midst of one for soccer, wanted an easel, paint & brushes, canvases and other supplies, so she could continue her artistic pursuit, for which she seems to have a passion. This is in addition to her weekly piano lessons.

Anna, while continuing her swimming lessons, wanted to learn how to play a musical instrument. A guitar, you say. Wrong. Piano? Nope. Drums? Eh eh. She asked her mom and dad for a violin! Not a lot of those in your average rock and roll group!

And her parents obliged.

Under any circumstances, this is cause for celebration. Like literally millions of other children, both girls play on soccer teams. They watch television, play with dolls, listen to music, go to the movies, love Disney characters. As a matter of fact, they both had their birthday parties at Disneyland. They love to laugh, make believe, and enjoy pizza and chocolate cupcakes. In other words, they enjoy the things that most normal seven year olds do. And still, they have an exuberant desire for engaging in the arts.

Without setting up a task force or committee, we should find out why. We should determine the magic elexir and sell it to others. No. Better yet, give it away, not by request, but secretly, maybe in the water alongside the fluoride, so our youngsters will have a passion for art that their parents cannot explain, since so few of our generation seem to care enough to promote. Or we could slip it into candy bars or McSnacks of all sorts. It could lead to a groundswell of art appreciation that could sweep the country. But I am getting ahead of myself. What potion do Kate and Anna share that made them interested in such esoteric pursuits?

I know the answer, because I am familiar with their parents. Larry & Nicky and Richard & Pam. None of them are in the arts. No actors. No musicians. No painters or writers. Just your everyday hardworking parents who simply make the arts available, along with sports and television and the rest, and then they encourage [not push]. I am pleased to be part of it all, the grandfather who bought the easel and the first violin lessons.

Availability. Encouragement. That's all it takes. The world of art is a world of wonder, where creativity abounds with the freedom of expression. With their built-in imaginations and their worlds of make believe, our children are naturally drawn to the arts. Given the opportunity, they will opt for some art form before almost anything else. Kids already have the magic potion running through their veins. Just point 'em in the right direct and kids will do the rest. All they need is the chance.

Learn to Eat Your Veggies

P eople like art and buy it for a variety of reasons. Everyone has a specific notion as to what art is and what it adds to their lifestyle. People buy art to decorate and beautify their homes or offices; others collect art for investment and to impress their friends or enhance their image to clients and peers. Still others buy for aesthetic satisfaction, and others are motivated by a combination of all the above. There are equally diverse opinions about what is good art and what is not.

It has been twenty years, but is as vividly planted in my mind as though it were yesterday, that a good client walked into my gallery in Gaithersburg, Maryland, and announced: *Yuk. Who did that piece of [expletive deleted]? It looks like twisted intestines. It's grotesque.* Her husband nodded vigorously in assent. Susan M. was referring to an original lithograph by Joan Miro, a significant twentieth century master. His works command ever-increasing prices, and he is represented in major museums around the world. Does that mean that Susan and Jack were wrong? I have quite a few friends who think that Miro's squiggles are nothing more than that--random wiggly lines. A woman once asserted, rather loudly, during an exhibit for 20th Century Masters in my D. C. gallery, *He's a Master? My five-year-old grand daughter can do that!*

These people are not wrong, nor are their opinions invalid. I happen to enjoy Miro's childlike imagery and playfulness, and his surrealistic philosophy. But if you don't like his art, it is irrelevant that Miro is "important." His historical significance is irrelevant to personal taste.

One of my closest friends thinks that historical importance matters a lot. He only deals in "important" artists and has little interest in people who buy art for decoration. I have a problem with the elitist view that only art by important artists is worth collecting. He contends that, if you buy something you like from a popular artist of the day, and the cost rivals that of a Master, you are stupid. *Dealers should educate people as to what is good and why it is important.* What happened to the idea of buying what you like? And so what if it's mainstream? Popularity should not be a requirement for determining if something is good, just as we should not rule out the possibility that something is good, simply because it is popular. The unmatched commercial success of the Beatles does not diminish their music.

I *LOVE* whatever I buy--a painting, a CD, a car, or a suit. And I do not need some self-appointed expert telling me how stupid I am--or, for that matter, how smart I am, based on the art I collect, what I drive or how well I dress.

So where does that leave you? Look around, and if you see something you like, buy it. And that's that. Well, maybe not. If you look at art as a "picture," and look for something pretty, your taste may be like an adult who never tasted food other than what he liked as a five-year-old. If I did not acquire a taste for the bitter and sour foods I hated as a kid, I would have missed out on Hunan lamb, asparagus, sweet and sour dishes, vinaigrette, and kosher pickles. I cannot imagine a worse punishment. Pretty pictures may be lovely to look at, sweet, like chocolate—or Fruit Loops. More developed art requires developing a taste for it, like adult food. As an art lover, don't grow up into one of those adults who don't like vegetables.

The next time you see a work of art you don't like, find something interesting about it, taste it, swish it around, give it a chance. You may never enjoy it, but you might learn to appreciate it. In the best of all worlds, you might come to love it, and find that the art you used to like is boring. You might want to try a spear of asparagus or a broccoli floret, even if you grew up not eating them.

Calling Liam Neeson and Alec Baldwin

Y ou probably have not heard of Tadeusz Lapinski. Then again, you might not have heard of Schindler, had it not been for Steven Spielberg. Not unlike Schindler, the life of Tadeusz Lapinski is the stuff of movies: Action. Danger. Excitement. Heart wrenching. Historic. Irony. Twists and turns. Redemption. Success. Tragedy. Renewal. Have I got your attention yet? Here are the details I can describe in about 700 words.

Born in Warsaw, Poland in 1928, Tadeusz was swept up in World War II. Scarcely a teenager, he became a member of Warsaw's Youth Underground, which fought the Nazis as best they could. The danger he faced grew, when his mother hid a Jewish baby in their home. Suspecting her but unable to find the child, the Nazis attempted to coerce her to give him up, by imprisoning young Tad. Each time they did, Tad escaped to continue the fight.

After the war, Lapinski pursued a career in art and was an immediate sensation. In 1960 he won the UNESCO First International Prize and the Olympic Art Award in Warsaw. In 1961, he was a prizewinner at the Cracow Biennial and won an award from the City of Radon. He followed that up with museum awards in Poland and Brazil in 1965 and 1967. Still, he yearned for more opportunity to express himself, to hurdle the Iron Curtain and present his art to the West. Leaving Poland was not an option, as the Communists ruled the country with an Iron Fist and were reluctant to lose one of their country's treasures.

In a rare twist of fate, one of the leaders of the Communist Party was the Jewish child the Lapinski family had saved. In a daring move, he enabled Tadeusz to escape to the West. I attempted to put that story out in 1981, but Tad begged me to suppress it, since his mother and sister were still in Poland, and he feared for their lives.

Lapinski arrived in Paris with his works in tow, and literally stumbled across the curator of the Museum of Modern Art, who was struck by his art and arranged an exhibition. Tad ended up in New York, where he taught at the Pratt Institute and had an exhibit at the Whitney Museum. He was quickly recognized for his printmaking virtuosity, versatility and innovation, and his art is now in the Museum of Modern Art in New York, the San Francisco Museum, the Philadelphia Museum, the Hirshhorn Museum and the Phillips Collection in Washington, D. C., the Jewish Museum, and the National Collection of Fine Arts. He is represented in over half a dozen museums in Yugoslavia and the Museums of Modern Art in Tokyo, Italy, and Brazil. He was the first American artist to have a one-man exhibition in mainland China [1985].

The journey was not easy. As fate would have it, while teaching at the University of Maryland in the early 1970's, he contracted aplastic anemia, a form of leukemia. Tad refused to quit—his art or his life. With great resolve and doctors, he overcame it!

I met Tad in the summer of 1979. I was visiting our Silver Spring, Maryland gallery, near the University. He came in with a number of pieces for framing. I did not know who he was, but admired the art. We struck up an instant friendship that has lasted to this day. I commissioned him to create a suite of four original lithographs. He produced four masterpieces, utilizing his special split rainbow technique. These were groundbreaking images, the most colorful of his career. Two years later, our flagship gallery was the home of a one-man show of Tad's works, and the Mayor gave him the key to the city, declaring December 9, 1981 as "Lapinski Day" in Washington, D. C. The mayor repeated the honor in 1982, in recognition of Lapinski's contribution to cultural life in the nation's capital.

What makes the art of Tadeusz Lapinski so special? He does it all himself, from the creation of the plates to the printing, which is painstakingly a piece at a time, a color at a time. His personal approach makes each piece unique. In addition to the remarkable achievement in colors, his works are further enhanced by his remarkable attainment of textures and layers. His imagery is modern, some works even futuristic, but his use of shapes and colors gives his art a universal appeal.

A brilliant artist. Freedom fighter. Teacher. Man of courage and purpose. Visionary. Inspiration. Tadeusz Lapinski has led the life of a legend and a hero. They should make a movie about him.

Liam Neeson looks like Tad and would be perfect for the part. If they need someone to play me in the movie, I am available if Alec Baldwin isn't.

Robert And Millie

S t. Boniface was less ornate than many churches I have been in, especially Catholic ones. Its high ceilings, richly colored and intricate, stained glass windows on the side walls, and the beautiful circular window at the rear of the church, contrasted with simple wooden pews and lack of monuments and sculptures. The Nativity Scene on the left hand side of the front stage was composed of innocent, naïf characters in ceramic. Poinsettias adorned the stage. Not much else. Simple. Warm. Uplifting, even for a non-Christian. Much like the synagogue I grew up attending in Southwest Washington, D. C.

Parishioners made their way into the church, their red faces outlined by scarves and hats, bodies bundled to protect them from the twelve degree Minneapolis weather. Familiar carols filled the room with soft background music, allowing participants to hum along, promoting the transition from the getting-and-spending world to the spiritual purpose of Christmas Mass. A soloist sang Silent Night [Heile Nacht] in German. Many in the growing assembly joined in, reminding me of how lovely people sound collectively when singing from the heart in a house of worship.

Growing up, I joined family and friends in belting out prayers in Hebrew. I had no idea what I was singing [I had not yet learned Hebrew], but I found the prayers inspiring. We place too much emphasis on reason and comprehension, even though they may not be important in spiritual settings. I remember sitting in the circle with Lakota [Sioux] friends. Their chanting combined into a collective mantra that evoked my personal spiritual beliefs. I have always found the Mass celebrated in Latin more inspirational than in English. Knowing what something means adds to the prayer. But it can also detract, if one is busy thinking about it too much, and it becomes like rote. Not understanding the words makes them vehicles for leaps of faith, just as great works of art and music can be uplifting. The carols sung in German added to the aura of St.

Boniface, founded by and for German immigrants a hundred years earlier.

I was awestruck by Millie Ladwig. At age 87, she climbed the steps into the sanctuary with great difficulty and resolve. Using her walker and help from her family, she made her way to the first pew, taking advantage of the caroling time before the Mass to regroup and regenerate. She did not come to watch. Or to listen. Or to simply be inspired. No, Millie came to participate, and participate she did. I could not hear her, although she was next to Patty, who was next to me. Soft spoken in ordinary circumstances, her frail voice was completely drowned out by the rest of us. But I could see her lips moving. She was singing along with the rest of us. No laggard. Not Millie. And not just the carols. As the Mass unfolded, during the responsive prayers, there she was, moving her lips, eyes closed. No need for the prayer book. The missal. Prayer is not about responsive reading. The very term, responsive reading, makes it just that. Don't read your prayers. Say them with feeling. Allow your spirit to soar with your thoughts of The Highest.

I remember looking at a prayer book that my father received from his brother, Max. The inscription was a masterpiece: "To Robert. Pray with kavannah. Love, Max." Kavannah is the Hebrew word for feeling. Uncle Max was reminding my dad to pray with feeling, with passion, not just recite the words. My father did, all of his life.

I especially remember one occasion when dad was ninety. It would be the last time we prayed together in public. Dad wasn't what he used to be, physically or in terms of mental alertness. You should know that, even during his peak years, dad could not hear well. We stood while the Cantor sang a prayer thanking God for all the gifts we have received from Him. It was the congregation's turn to join in, to add our personal and collective thanks. Dad had been quiet since we arrived. He looked at his prayer book, most of the time with his eyes shut. He knew all the prayers by heart. Occasionally, his body moved. It could not have been more than five or ten seconds into the prayer. Dad heard it as the rest of us belted in out. And then his lips began to move. And then, he began to sing with the rest of us, always a beat behind, even as he had been for the fifty years I prayed with him. His eyes closed, his body moving rhythmically to prayer, his face lit by the Light from within. He sang with Kavannah! I believe I prayed with more Kavannah that night than I had previously or have since.

Robert and Millie. Two people separated by religion and ritual, clearly joined by faith and spirit. I am blessed to have been in their presence during their finest moment.

The Heart of Art

*T*hese columns are concerned with the relationship between art and Society, covering such topics as conflicts, funding, censorship, the role of art, political ramifications, and art education & our schools.

C'mon Rudy,
You Know Better

O nce again there is a raging debate about what is art and whether a government has the right to decide what can or cannot be displayed in public areas, as well as who should pay for it. At the center of the controversy is New York City Mayor Rudy Giuliani. The art in question is an exhibition of African Art at the Brooklyn Museum.

The mayor believes that the art is an affront to Christians and wants the exhibit closed. Mayor Rudy is well aware of the First Amendment and knows that he cannot prevent the exhibition simply because he does not like the art, or, for that matter, is offended by it. The truth is, he wants the exhibit taken down because he does find it offensive. So he is suing the museum for misuse of public funds, since taxes are a significant part of the funding required to mount the exhibit. He seems oblivious to Chief Justice James Rehnquist's observation that Government does not have the right to prohibit or censor anything because they are offended by it.

What about the art? The current brouhaha is over a painting which depicts the Virgin Mary in an unkindly light, exacerbated by her torso being 'painted' with elephant dung in the mixture. Other works include dead animal body parts floating in formaldehyde and other controversial imagery. People are picketing and protesting in front of the museum, some for, others against the exhibit. Most of them have not seen it, simply exercising their right to protest on either side of the issue.

The reaction by those who have seen the exhibit is mixed. Based on 'exit polls' about a third enjoyed the art, some even using words like inspiring and beautiful to describe it. Another third did not like it at all. The remaining third were neutral. All were glad that they had the opportunity to see it. None were offended.

The broader question seems to escape Mayor Rudy and other self-appointed art critic/social arbiters. Censorship, by any other name, smells bad. In the 1980's an exhibit of Robert Mapplethorpe's photography became the subject of public outcry by politicians, especially those with a conservative bent. The National Endowment for the Arts underwrote the exhibition, which featured photographs of explicit homosexual activity. No one criticized the artistic, aesthetic or technical accomplishments of the artist. Only his subject matter. Protestors said it was vulgar, blasphemous, shocking, dangerous for our children to see, etc.

The show was canceled. I saw a catalog of the art in question. I found the graphic explicitness of some of the imagery distasteful. Wouldn't want it in my house. I was impressed with the composition, use of light, boldness, and much of the art was provocative, forcing me to face certain realities I might have otherwise ignored. Art enables us examine our society, our mores and traditions. A lot of people can't handle that. As a result, Mark Twain's *Tom Sawyer* and *The Adventures of Huckleberry Finn* are banned from some school systems, on the basis they are racist. No matter that they accurately depict a society a lot of us are not proud of, and would rather forget. Several of William Shakespeare's plays have also been banned because of their subject matter. For example, the young promiscuous love and the complicity of suicide in *Romeo and Juliet* are raging issues.

If you attend a play or movie that you find distasteful, you have right to get up and leave. You do not have right to prevent others from staying. The melting pot of America gives us the opportunity to learn about others with whom we share this ever-shrinking planet. Nothing describes culture better than art. Not that art needs justification. Art for art's sake is an important concept in a free society. In the long run, art mirrors society, the good and the bad. Both views deserve equal opportunity to be examined.

Allow governments to decide what is acceptable, and you allow them to shield personal values of incumbents. Worse yet, you give them the ability insulate themselves from public scrutiny.

Suppose a book was critical of our government. Should our government have the right to prevent it from being available to the public?

Censorship is insidious. Governments convolute our freedoms to protect themselves. In the 1950's, secret cameras photographed citizens attending the Bolshoi Ballet and Moussoyev Dance Troupe at the National Theater in Washington, D. C. Senator Joseph McCarthy and his cohorts decided that any Americans who enjoyed Russian music and dance were security risks. Speaking of Russia, writers Boris Pasternak [*Doctor Zhivago*] and Aleksander Solzhenitsyn [*The First Circle* and *One Day in the Life of Ivan Denisovich*] were imprisoned and their books banned because of derogatory views about communism, and, in Solzhenitsyn's case, for remarks about Stalin.

Let's not even begin to go down that path.

Hooray for Michelangelo

A friend of mine took exception to my column, which criticized Mayor Rudy Giuliani for his attempting to censor the art exhibition, which included distasteful [to some people] depictions of Christian Symbolism. John wrote, "Artists want it both ways. They'll take public money but not conform to *our* standards." Whose standards are "our" standards? They are not mine. They are Giuliani's. Many of the people who think the government should dictate taste to the rest of us have never demonstrated great taste. Would you buy or wear the ties that Strom Thurmond does? Some look like they were cut out of remnants of a Confederate flag. And what about the way he combs his hair? Ditto for most of the old geezers who set themselves up as our moral arbiters of art.

Just as our forefathers foresaw the need to separate Church and State, there should be a separation of Art and State, based on the notion "they" cannot tell me what's right or good. That does not mean that artists should not be accountable for their use of public funds. But the public should decide. I don't like where all my tax dollars go. Maybe a little less on weapons of destruction, a little more on education and art. Other citizens have their pet peeves and projects. We don't have to like all the art we fund. A panel comprised of citizens from various walks of life, who also know something about art, could be our jury, in a sense. Wait! We have that. Well, we HAD that. We called it the National Endowment of the Arts, the scapegoat of conservative thinkers, who took away its funds. Ironically, these are often the same people who advocate less government control and interference. Their outrage is over art that offends them, even as they coddle gun manufacturers and fight against keeping guns out of the hands of our children. I consider that misguided outrage.

The first recorded act of censorship that I could find happened in Italy about five hundred years ago. Based on the premise that whoever pays for the art knows what is good taste, or at least has bought the right to dictate what is acceptable, the Pope told Michelangelo to put a fig leaf on Adam's private parts. Mikey resisted, telling the Pope that His Holiness could paint it on if he wanted Adam covered. Besides, in the Old Testament, God created Man without any covering. Adam doesn't wear a fig leaf until after the apple-eating incident in the Garden of Eden.

There is another current hot topic related to the notion of censorship and protecting the First Amendment rights of artists, including musicians and moviemakers. Some members of Government want to get those artists to regulate themselves. Some of my friends in the arts are screaming censorship and the violation of their First Amendment rights. Sorry, guys, but the issue is not about censorship or the First Amendment. Does it violate the First Amendment rights of Philip Morris by forbidding them to sponsor Sesame Street? And what about the showing of a sexually explicit film as part of an after-school afternoon series? Is it censorship to tell the Colt Company that they can't give out cardboard samples of their guns during recess, or advertise them on billboards across the street from a public school? Would it bother you if Anheuser Bush sponsored Barney and Friends? And how do you feel about the showing of *Goodfellas* or *Pulp Fiction* instead of cartoons on Saturday morning TV? Why aren't you screaming about the rights of those industries? Because their rights are not being violated. "We the People" don't want those products pushed on to our kids during their formative, vulnerable years. And remember that, just as you cannot yell "FIRE!" in a movie theater if there isn't one, not every restriction of what you can say and where you can say it is a First Amendment right violation.

Make your porno flicks, or "adult theme" movies, show all the violence you want, say or sing whatever vulgarities turn you on. Just don't surreptitiously market those products to innocent eleven-year-olds. Or to my grandchildren. Show them to yours, if it suits you, but I insist that you put my Katie, Anna and Daniel above your wallets. That, my friends, is not censorship. It is responsible citizenship.

The Ripple Effect

E ver since the Pope commissioned Michelangelo to paint the Sistine Chapel, people of money and influence have supported and nurtured the arts. Early on, the Medici sponsored their favorite artists, resulting in some of the most incredible and enduring art man has ever produced. In the late nineteenth and twentieth centuries, notable American entrepreneurs, such as Mellon, Carnegie, Guggenheim, Hirshhorn, and Freer, supported and collected their favorite artists, resulting in major museums which give the rest of us the opportunity to enjoy, to be nurtured by, the beauty and spirit of art. The tradition is ongoing, but you get my point.

The contribution of art to society is unmistakable. The pleasure it brings us is complemented by the intellectual challenge it can provide. And all that is magnified by the double-headed concept that, on the one hand, art mirrors and chronicles society, while on the other, it anticipates society's direction and future. A recent phenomenon has expanded the value and purpose of art, in a way that the artists never imagined. Art has reached the highest plateau.

Instead of donating art to museums, some art collectors donate their art to universities, hospitals and various charities. One such example touches my heart. In the Washington, D. C. Metropolitan Area, there is an organization called The Good Knight Campaign. It was established about ten years ago, with the expressed goal of teaching children how to stay out of harm's way, how to avoid abduction, violence and victimization. Its books, programs, activities and videos are primarily aimed at children 5 & up. My grandchildren have seen the videos. So should yours. I am honored to be a "knight" for some help I gave when the *Good Knight* came to Los Angeles and visited several elementary schools. When you are in the D. C. Area, you might want to plan a visit to the Good Knight Angelic Kingdom, a 2+ acre Museum of Modern Mythology & Gardens, located in Beltsville, MD. If yours is a family trip, put the visit high on your agenda. Family activities include classes and activities devoted to teaching children how to protect themselves.

Several art collectors I know have donated art to this special organization, and they would be pleased to know that their generosity is serving the community in a way they might not have imagined. In order to expand their programs to help empower the next generation, the Charity is selling the art to other art lovers and corporations interested in helping their cause. It is likely that the artists themselves did not imagine the impact their vision could have on our children. Even the 20th century master, Salvador Dali, with an ego as big as all outdoors, and whose works are being sold by the Charity, could not have predicted the expansive nature of his art. The funds raised will enable the Charity to place funds into their crime and prevention programs. Maestro Dali would be pleased!

Rather than sell art that you no longer want, why not give it to a worthy cause? If you want to help our children, The Good Knight Campaign is one of my favorites [visit www.goodknight.org for more info.]. Children's Hospital in Los Angeles is another. A different cause may be close to your heart. Who you help is not as important as helping. There are no bad choices.

Conversely, if you are interested in collecting art, look for a charity that has some for sale. When you buy art from a charity, you start an endless chain reaction.

A work of art donated to a charity is like a stone dropped into a still lake. First, it brings beauty into the world. That is the first ripple. It also reflects our society--past, present and future. Ripple number two. When sold by the charity, it brings money to that organization, which enables it to serve all of us. Ripple number three. As their generosity serves that broader purpose, those who donated the art receive the joy of giving. That's Ripple number four. Then there is the beauty and pleasure brought into the lives of those who buy art from charities. Ripple number five. Finally, the act of buying the art from a charity brings a satisfaction to those end users, who, as they enjoy the art, recognize that their money will help a greater cause, such as preventing child abuse or finding the cure for a dreaded disease. Ripple number six. Each worthwhile purpose achieved is a wider circle than the previous one. One could say that the value of art to our society is unlimited.

Those who would continue to diminish art programs in schools need to sit by a lake and look at the ripples.

Maybe Mona's Laughing at Us

F or years, long before Nat King Cole immortalized her mystic smile in pop culture, Mona Lisa was the subject of controversy and widespread speculation and interpretation. Why the smile? Is it really a self-portrait of Leonardo Da Vinci, disguised as a woman? Was there a hidden message in that notion? And so on. Unfortunately, based on everything I have read, Leo didn't tell anyone or leave any clues for future generations. We are on our own.

Academics and recognized and self appointed experts enjoy the mental gymnastics of interpreting art for the rest of us, from poetry to literature to music to visual art. I have a problem with that notion on two fronts. One, have they been given some divine inspiration or has the artist explained things to them in a dream? And, two, if the answers to "Question One" are not "yes," why can't the rest of us figger it out? What makes them smarter than the rest of us? Or what makes them *think* they're smarter.

That does not mean that art cannot be interpreted, based on available information, either from the artist or those who knew him or her. For example, Salvador Dali, the 20th century surrealist master, utilized color and numerology in his art. There are many books written on both subjects, so an art historian has the tools available to interpret "hidden meanings" in Dali's paintings. When no such information is available, and no clues are left by the artist, the question of interpretation becomes moot.

When I read Dante's Divine Comedy in college, I read various interpretations on that masterpiece. Several "authorities" asserted that the *COMEDY* was written on seven levels. I have always had a problem with that pronouncement. The very word "levels" implies a hierarchy of messages, so the mundane folk understand the basic story, or what's in the basement. Anything else, they need people smarter than they are to explain it to them. And it gets more and more difficult as it reaches the rarified air of higher levels.

More likely, experts were aware of seven opinions of the meaning of the epic. Those who came up with the seventh interpretation automatically assumed that it must be a higher intellectual achievement, since no one else had reached that rarified place. Of course, if you and I had our own explanations, that would raise the bar to eight or nine levels. Except that our opinions don't count! Perhaps Dante had just one thing in mind when he wrote it—one level—and all the rest is idle speculation.

Have you ever had a portrait photo shoot for you or someone in your family? How do you finally pick out the one to blow up and frame? There are a number of criteria you could apply in making your final selection. If it is a group photo, you could choose the one in which the most people look good. Or you could choose the one that flatters you the most, as opposed to the one which most looks like you. After all, rank has its privilege. The photograph that is blown up and framed for future generations to see becomes "history." Does that mean it is the one that most accurately captures how everyone looked? Maybe not.

Moreover, are there hidden meanings that future generations could argue over. Do they find some hidden meaning in "Aunt Tillie's twisted smile?" Or does "Uncle Vanya's foreboding look" imply that he was secretly spying or committing some other crime?

The point is that art is subject to interpretation. That does not mean that the various interpretations represent levels, all of which were in the artist's mind from the beginning. In our recent pop culture, the song, *Strawberry Fields Forever,* from the Beatles' album, "Sergeant Pepper's Band" supposedly had a secret message. If played at the wrong speed, some people asserted that there was a message that Paul McCartney was dead. And on the cover of the Abbey Road album, the four Beatles were walking across the street, but Paul was out of step. Another secret message that he was dead? Wrong on all counts. Along those same lines, did the song, "Lucy in the Sky with Diamonds" refer to LSD?

Those who act like they are in the know pontificate what the hidden meanings are in everything. The same kind of attitude is pervasive in our society. There are those among us who ascribe a conspiracy theory to everything.

Meanwhile, I get the strange feeling that Mona is laughing at us.

But Is It a Duck?

I f it quacks, waddles, swims, has wings but can't fly; if it has a first name like "Peking" or "Donald" and such last names as "a L'Orange" and "Montmerancy;" it's probably a duck. Some things are easy to identify. It used to be that way with art. I doubt that anyone looking at Leonardo's "Last Supper" or "Mona Lisa" or any of Monet's "water lilies" paintings would not consider them art. You don't have to like all art. Frankly, the "Mona Lisa" doesn't do anything for me. But it IS art. So is Van Gogh's "Starry Night," Salvador Dali's melting clocks and Andy Warhol's soup cans.

The twentieth century may be remembered as the Century of the Atom—Time Magazine chose Einstein as the Man of the Century. It could also be remembered as the Century of Freedom, as the proliferation of new nations spewed forth in great numbers because people around the world wanted out from their yokes of oppression. Freedom. The elixir of change. The demand for less boundaries and convention.

Poetry lost the need for rhyme or rhythm. Music became dissonant. Four Four and Three Four Time were joined by 5/7 and other never-before-tried tempos and rhythms. Even songs already written, were performed with "artistic license," with scat vocals and variations in contrast with the melody, as jazz reared its head and announced itself as the freedom of expression in music.

Much of what was first considered "bad" or "wrong" is perfectly acceptable in the art world. I wonder if that is because of critical acceptance, which led to public consumption and acceptance; or critics caving in to the weight of mass acceptance. It probably works in both directions. In music, soul, country, rock 'n roll, even jazz, had their cult followings long before their stars received critical acclaim. As those followings expanded, the pressure became too great for critics not to take notice, and ultimately acquiesce. The likes of Elvis, The Beatles, Ella, and Garth became household names.

Walt Whitman's *Leaves of Grass* was controversial poetry not well received by 19th century experts, yet it is pretty tame stuff compared to the non-rhythmic poetry of today.

What about hip-hop? Grunge? Harder than hard metal? Screaming singers? Is it music? Are the performers artists? Careful if your from-the-hip answer is a resounding NO. It may be a generational thing, or it may be a cultural difference, since we are all more comfortable with the tried and true of our personal cultural experiences. That's why your parents told you to turn down that noise when you played rock 'n roll in the 50's and 60's. Now the best of that music are considered classics. And what about the brake dancing from the streets? Remember when it wasn't considered dancing? Now, the best of that has also worked its way into modern dance in musical productions and the repertoire of avant-garde dance troupes.

How about a pile of debris and trash in the corner of a room? There are artists doing that, insisting that they are making a statement about life or society, or something or other. Is it art? Frankly, I have a problem identifying a pile of rubble as art. When I took out my trash last night and dumped it with several neighbors' unwanted garbage, I did not step back and decide it reminded me of a work of art and should be shown in a gallery. Am I prejudiced? Narrow-minded? Too sheltered an environment to understand the plight of our society and the role some artists have accepted to articulate it to the rest of us? Besides, if a pile of trash were a work of art, my parents would tell you I was creating masterpieces in my room fifty years ago.

I don't know. What IS creativity and what, if any, are its limitations? I can only safely say what I like and don't like, and the rest of you can agree or disagree. It's all a matter of choice, isn't it?

Okay, then. That pile of trash I saw a picture of in Art News Magazine a while back—they can call it what they want. To me, it looked like a picture of a pile of trash. If it gets into a museum, they had better rope it off. Otherwise, some cleaning lady is going to throw away a masterpiece.

Baseball Bats
vs.
Paint Brushes

I'm worried about where we are headed from a cultural standpoint. Common threads running through science fiction stories fuel my concern.

The emphasis is on technological development. Gadgets, robots, space ships, and other inventions reflect the unbridled imaginations of writers. Set designers show "futuristic" looks in furniture, while fashion designers take a similar approach to costuming, outfitting the actors in togas or body suits which look derivative of surfer wet suits. The music is usually synthesized music. Outside the writing, the threads are woven into the narrowest of tapestries, as utilitarian and functional considerations far outweigh aesthetic ones. In a not so subtle style, we are being told that, in the future, the value of art will be nil. To make matters worse, do you ever see art on the walls? Or hear music played by real orchestras and instruments? The message is, why bother with something that has no apparent value? There is rarely a reference to art, or a character bemoaning the lack of it.

What makes the scenario more jarring is that science fiction has been a barometer in predicting the future. Artists tell us where we, as a society, are headed. Leonardo daVinci and Jules Verne exemplify how the science fiction of yesterday becomes the reality of today. The artists who paint a bleak artistic picture may be giving us a wakeup call as to our priorities and direction.

There is reason for hope. It is difficult to get a seat to the opera in any major city in America. Museum attendance is at an all time high and increasing annually. The United States actually had the three most attended museum shows in the world in 1999. It may be too little too late. We do little in our society to nurture the arts. Politicians use them as a political football, discarding their importance in budget allocation. What better to cut than money from programs that have a tiny voice in the arena of public opinion? The arts don't have much of an advocacy that politicians need to appease.

Donations to politicians by people in the arts hardly compare to corporate or other special interest investments. Ironically, when artists who have made a lot of money donate to candidates who reflect their views, the media and opponents vilify both the recipients and the artists. I wonder if the politicians who advocate discarding art programs such as the National Endowment for the Arts are not really posturing, in an attempt to win over voters with their frugality. They know the risk of voter reprisal is minimal. Members of Congress from my generation must remember taking required classes in art and music in high school. Maybe these guys love art, but pretend they don't for political expediency.

It is fine to promote physical fitness, but to promote athletic programs in our schools at the expense of art programs is to treat our kids as simply physical beings. We should nurture the imaginations of our children, and encourage them to create and enjoy beauty as much as strength and physical fitness. Put computers in every classroom, but why not pipe in great music while our kids learn technical skills? We stress computer literacy and bemoan the lack of reading ability among students at virtually all levels. The contrast by generation is clear. People my age, as a group, are not nearly as good on the computer as our children and grandchildren, and I have no problem with that. I am concerned that my grandchildren may never read Shakespeare, Tolstoy, Shaw, or Fitzgerald.

While I'm standing on my soapbox, I want to shout out some of the pragmatic values of the arts. They preserve ethnic cultures that, in America, provide the opportunity for an incredibly rich tapestry, which describes our diversity and our power. They provide creative outlets and the opportunity for creative expression to preserve cultures. And while we have a multiple-language society evolving in America, art overcomes the boundaries of languages. The popularity of Latino music is a testament to that notion.

I am amazed at the number of people who return from trips abroad, in awe of the great art they saw. If you are one of them, time to look homeward, angels, so that, in years to come, people who travel to the United States return to their homelands equally impressed by our art and culture.

It's Time to Draw the Line

*H*e looked liked an angel. Hard to believe that an hour earlier he was perpetual motion. The Everready Bunny. A three-foot tall thirty-five pound two and half year old bundle of laughter, racing helterskelter through the house. A bundle of energy. E=MC squared. Mr. Excitement. Not now. He was quiet as a lamb, lying spread eagled on his bed, his face the picture of contentment. Oh, yeah, Daniel was definitely an angel. Meanwhile, strains of a familiar Mozart ditty from *Eine Kleine Nacht Musik* filled his room.

After filling myself to the brim with the joy and beauty of the moment, I left my grandson's room and congratulated my son, Richard, for playing Mozart at Daniel's bedtime. Richard nodded and assured me that Daniel also went to sleep hearing Beethoven, Schubert, Tchaikovsky, the Beatles, Sting, and a wide range of jazz and rock and roll.

"We want him to love it all, dad. And he already does! That puts him about twenty years ahead of me."

Pam [my daughter-in-law] and Richard also have a houseful of art, from paintings by people you never heard of—well, at least I haven't—to a few lithographs by Joan Miro, a few posters of works by Masters, to some amazing creations by my five year old granddaughter, Anna. Eclectic. Not too serious. Definitely exposing their kids to art.

I am gratified. I am concerned about the demise of art in our culture. Even the most upscale homes are often devoid of art, save an occasional color-coordinated over-the-sofa innocuous painting, often chosen by a decorator. My motto is: If you want to decorate your house, buy pillows. Art should harmonize with your soul, not your sofa.

I can't remember the last time I went into a home and heard music playing, unless it was a jingle blaring from the television set. Years ago, at a small dinner party at my home, one guest complained that the background music was annoying, while another, after dinner, asked where the TV set was, so he could hear the news. A far cry from the time I had Tadeusz Lapinski, an artist friend of mine from Warsaw, Poland, and his wife for dinner. I put on a CD, and within a minute, the two of them exclaimed: "Chopin. His Third Scherzo." And a moment later: "Richter!" They were referring to Sviatoslav Richter, the Russian pianist. They explained that they had stood in a freezing rain for hours to get tickets to his concert in Warsaw in the late 1950's.

All the arts are in trouble. The reason there are so many revivals of great dramas on Broadway is that no one will risk money on a new play. Arthur Miller, whose *Death of a Salesman* has enjoyed a remarkable second life, says that he would never be able to get it produced if he wrote it today.

If we are not going to teach our children about the arts in school, the home becomes the last line of defense. The Maginot Line. Dunkirk. The Charge of the Light Brigade. Our goal-line stand. You have the opportunity—and the obligation—to be Bill Russell against the fast break, John Elway in the fourth quarter, and Babe Ruth in the bottom of the ninth. If you don't do it, our team loses. You. Me. Kids. Society.

Art lovers of the world, unite! Throw down your TV's. Unshackle yourselves from the yoke of oppression that values the inane over the artistic; money over taste; brash over beauty.

I hear a lot of people complain about the athletes who sign $50 million, even a hundred million dollar contracts. Don't complain. You're to blame. When I take Katie [my other perfect 5 year old granddaughter] to the park after her ballet class, I hear parents telling their kids they can be the next Michael Jordan, Pete Sampras or Tiger Woods—or their female counterparts. Sorry, I'm not as up on women's sports. Okay. Venus Williams or Anika Somebody. What about the next Picasso? Or Scott Joplin? Or Lillian Hellman? Or Itzhak Pearlman? Or Maya Angalou?

Folks, if you don't like the way things are going in our society, stop complaining. Do something about it.

An Idyllic Discovery

*T*his has been a wonderful year for me as an art lover. Regional theaters are enjoying a resurgence across the country. Granddaughters Katie and Anna are taking music lessons—Katie now in her second year on piano, Anna just beginning on the violin. And just this past weekend I attended a jazz festival in Idyllwild, California, an annual event to support the Music & Art Academy nestled in the pines. The population of Idyllwild is 2,200. More people than that attended the two-day event.

I stayed in a lodge a mile from Idyllwild, in a place called Pine Cove. The owner/operator has eclectic interests. When he is not running the lodge, he lectures on astronomy [the skies above Idyllwild, which is 6,000 feet above sea level, are clear and star-studded]. When he is not star gazing, Gary is a percussionist in the Inland Valley Symphony Orchestra, a 50-piece group of dedicated and talented musicians. Gary lent me a CD that I listened to driving around the beautiful countryside. Working in anonymity and for the love of the music, these fifty musicians offered up a highly professional rendition of Rachmaninoff's *Rhapsody on a Theme by Paganini*. The featured pianist, local Dr. Corey Bell, did himself proud, too, on one of my favorite tunes in the classical repertoire. I am planning to walk down the aisle to one of its melodies at my upcoming wedding. I was sincerely moved by the music. The orchestra doesn't have to apologize for the next piece on the CD either: Beethoven's Fifth Symphony, delivered with power and style, and also highly polished. I did not get to hear the third piece on the CD, Rimsky-Korsikov's *Capricio Espanol*, an equally ambitious undertaking.

I stumbled across at least four art galleries in town, which displayed everything from contemporary paintings to blown glass, to a range of Native American art objets. There are also numerous fine restaurants offering gourmet food in charming settings. No, I am not a member of the local chamber of commerce [I am not sure they even have one]. It is just refreshing to discover and then report to you about a cultural Mecca in a place you might least suspect. Just last week, a columnist for the New York Times was lamenting the woes of culture and the arts—that they are elitist and out of reach of the common folk. He should visit Idyllwild, California.

But the diamond in the rough is the school. One of three boarding arts high schools in the United States, the Idyllwild Arts Academy offers pre professional training in the arts along with a rigorous college-preparatory academic curriculum. The school includes grades 8-12. Students are selected for admission by audition or portfolio evaluation, along with their academic history and transcripts. Over half the students enrolled receive financial aid from the school totaling more than $2 million annually. What and experience for the kids! Nurturing their creative spirit in an idyllic location, side by side with kids from 14 countries outside the U. S. and 22 states besides California. The Summer Arts Program caters to 1,300 students each year, including children, junior and high school students, and adults and college students. If they have and pursue dreams in the arts, perhaps Katie and Anna could attend the Academy in ten years, and learn from a distinguished faculty of artist-educators.

As for the jazz festival, my friend, Ernie Watts, saxophonist supreme, played on Saturday afternoon. His quartet included an extraordinary drummer, and another friend, Bob Leatherbarrow. They played in the outdoor amphitheater, before appreciative jazz enthusiasts who sat on blankets and folding chairs, protected from the sun by large parachutes, strung together as a giant canopy. Forest rangers rode their horses along the trails surrounding the venue, and the large pines that encircled the theater cast moving shadows through the parachutes, as the sun ambled across the sky. What a beautiful experience. Outside the theater, which was the largest of the three venues, more than fifty artists presented their arts and crafts. Musicians, painters, potters, sculptors, jewelry makers, you name it.

Art supporting the arts. What could be better? Not much.

And I feel a lot better about our society than I have in quite a while. I am constantly bombarded with examples of the demise of the arts in our culture. It was quite fulfilling to find art alive and well and living under the stars among the pines in Idyllwild. It is gratifying to know that the students at that Academy are artists-in-training who will bring beauty in the world tomorrow. I will sleep better knowing that.

See that Van Gogh

S everal friends saw the Picasso exhibition at the LA County
Museum before I did. The consensus was that the exhibit
was nothing special, a view shared by the art critic of a major local
newspaper. I did not let their views deter me from going. A good
thing, too.

The first room contained the 1905 black & white etching, *The
Frugal Repast*. This print is pure magic. I stood in front of it for
nearly ten minutes, mesmerized by its pathos, its despair, the sense
of hopelessness, resignation and indifference expressed by the old
couple. Picasso's technique produced textures, depth, richness
and nuances rarely seen in gravures. Perhaps in a Rembrandt, maybe
a Goya, maybe not.

I thoroughly enjoyed the exhibit. *Woman with Guitar*, a 1922
painting, leaped off the canvas, its subtle colors, shifting focus and
diffused, fragmented imagery, anticipating the Surrealists that
followed. It could easily have been painted in the 1990's by a
contemporary artist, and be considered "art of today." There
were several portraits that Picasso painted between the ages of 10
and 13. They were remarkable achievements of color and balance,
not for a prepubescent, but for an artist of any age. A number of
black & white etchings from the late 1920's and early '30's
displayed the elegance, simplicity of line, spark of spontaneity,
and delicious satirical humor that are distinctly *Picasso!*
Sculptures in bronze, wood and terra cotta were scattered
throughout the exhibit. I liked them all. My companion shared my
enthusiasm, although we had different favorites.

Was this the same exhibit that my friends attended?   Perhaps
they were comparing it with earlier, larger Picasso exhibits, with
more of his famous works. They lost sight of what was there. In
later conversations, it turned out they liked it more than they
thought.

It's a sign of the times: bigger is better; loud dominates softly;

color overshadows black and white; technically complex beats simplicity. The dominant movie of 1998 at the box office and at the Academy Awards was *Titanic*, compared with *On the Waterfront* in 1951 and *Marty* in 1954. From movies to Broadway, in music and in art, we are obsessed with the notion that spectacle and size are the standards of excellence. Even the proliferation of animated feature length movies acquiesces to technology, at the expense of true emotional grit.

Critics applaud "small" movies with adult themes, singling them out for their rarity. They are often overshadowed by big films, like a small brownstone surrounded by skyscrapers. I prefer Charlton Heston's *Moses* to the animated character in *Prince of Egypt*, cared more for Charles Laughton's *Quasimoto*, than the cartoon hunchback, and enjoy Picasso's small pieces as much as his larger, more famous ones. They can elicit equally powerful and satisfying viewer responses.

Now for that art critic. He has the right to pan whatever he doesn't like. It's his job. Only he forgot to do it. Rather than review the art, he reviewed the exhibit as an event, compared it to a prior one and complained about what was missing.

So what? What about people who have never seen an original Picasso and rely on that critic for guidance? Did he consider that some might not attend? Responsibility accompanies the power to influence. That critic failed to tell us what the Picasso Exhibit did have to offer, thereby depriving people from seeing what he considers "second tier" Picasso's. So what if a hundred masterpieces were absent? What if there were "only" six masterpieces and dozens of other wonderful rare works by the artist of the century? I enjoy showing friends etchings by Picasso, and they enjoy seeing them.

The Van Gogh Exhibit is next at LACMA. When I was on the East Coast, several people said that, *"these aren't the most famous Van Gogh's, so I was disappointed."* I would hope that the same art critic reviews what is in the show, not what's missing.

Whatever you hear or read, don't miss it. Van Gogh's color, passion and despair are prevalent in all of his art, so it doesn't matter if these are his most famous paintings. Pack your kids in the family van and go. You may never have another opportunity to see Van Gogh paintings. Be your own art critic. After all, who knows better than you what you like? And your kids won't know what they are missing.

The Years Are Passing By

I recently completed a three-month stint at sea, giving art lectures and conducting art auctions aboard a very upscale cruise ship. The auctions consisted primarily of unknown artists with a sprinkling of pieces by a few household names. I was struck by the number one question from passengers: *Is this a good investment?*

I understand why they ask the question. They have been led to believe that the most popular art is a good investment. Who told them? Art auctioneers at sea? Yes! I have heard them do it. Most of them have no art background. Their previous work experiences, with some notable exceptions, range from photographers on ships to radio and sports personalities to cruise staffers. Who else spreads the word to buy art? Art "consultants" [euphemism for salespeople] in art galleries? For sure. They present the most popular names of the day as investment opportunities. They point to the rising prices of works by these artists. They point to "sold out editions" and secondary market prices. I have also seen art dealers on the Financial News Network recommend buying emerging artists, whose works might sell for a few hundred dollars, as long term investments. Not as far as I am concerned. Let me tell you why.

Let's deal with the last assertion first, buying a piece of art by an unknown artist for a few hundred dollars for a long-term investment. Could it become a winner for you? Of course. Digging deeply in your front yard could make you rich, too, if you strike oil. Or winning the lottery. And the odds are not all that different. Hey, if you see a piece of art that strikes your fancy and it costs a few hundred dollars, buy it. But buy it because you like it. It's probably never going to be worth anything, except the pleasure it brings you. And that's enough.

As for the popular artists of the day, how would we know if their works would be popular in the future? Or that there would even be a market for their works? Think about writers or musicians who were popular years ago, and who nobody reads or listens to today. Does that make the art bad? Of course not. Just remember, buy art because you like it—rather, because you *love* it. If it turns out to be a good investment, that's a bonus.

Even then, how many of us would sell something we enjoy because we could make a few bucks on it? I have sold art to numerous clients who contend that they bought it for investment as much as pleasure of having it on their walls. Yet, when I provide them with updated appraisals and they see that their art has appreciated, not client has ever called and asked me to sell the art for a profit. They do seem to get added pleasure knowing that they made a "good investment" decision. Several enjoy announcing to their friends what they paid for their art and what it is currently worth.

Then there are those people who do not understand the notion of putting a dollar value on art. Not because they are stupid or naïve, mind you, but because they put a higher value on it. The young [mid-twenties] stewardess who cleaned my cabin is such a person. She is from Budapest, Hungary, and she works on ships six months at a time, takes a month off and goes at it again, making beds, cleaning toilets, and providing the best personal service she can to an often-demanding group of people. She asked me if I had any books on artists or art history. "I can't afford to buy art, and since I began working on ships," she exclaimed, " I have little time for visiting museums or enjoying art in public places, like I used to do with my friends at the university."

"I have several books I'll loan you," I replied. *"Great!"* she exclaimed. *"The years are passing by."* Too bad she does not have the money to buy art.

Art is the mirror of our society, of whom we are, where we have been, and often of where we are going. That is what makes it fun as well as fascinating, instructive as well as pretty, satisfying as well as decorative. I hope the time will come, Eszther, that you will be able to collect art. You love it for all the right reasons.

Ready, Set, Paint!

*M*ore financial pressure on the states means more pressure on local governments. More pressure on local governments means one of two things: less government services or higher local taxes. Of course, there is reluctance to raise taxes in a fragile economic environment coming out of a recession. The risk is the dreaded "double dip" recession if consumers find their disposable income shrinking. All this because of impending federal tax cuts and shifting the incidence of responsibility from federal to state levels.

Why should the economy be a topic of a column on the arts? Because, unfortunately, in a society where squeaky wheels get the oil, the arts don't have much of a united constituency. At the national level, the National Endowment for the Arts disintegrated under the weight of balanced budgets, defense spending, law enforcement, and other pressing issues. And as states battled to keep their heads above water, school budgets are under enormous pressure, and programs on the arts take a back seat to teachers' salaries, campus security, maintenance, books, and just about everything else. If there were to be less teachers, who goes first, the science or math teacher, or the art or music teacher? That is a "no-brainer" in this society.

If learning about the arts took a back seat to readin', writin' and 'rithmetic, I would not only understand, I would be at the forefront applauding. If the arts came in behind campus security, I would lead the charge. After all, safety first for Katie and Anna, my two perfect granddaughters, and Daniel, my perfect grandson. Well-maintained classrooms, adequate supplies, whatever it takes for them to get the education they deserve, hey, let's do it. I will lead the shouting of grandparents everywhere, bellowing out the need to educate our kids' kids.

But wait. What about eliminating exposure to the arts altogether, taking away art appreciation and involvement, even one or two days a week? That scares me. And when budgets include every sport that can be played with various size balls and sticks, indoors and outdoors, that scares me more. I hasten to add that I appreciate the valuable lessons of sports and could list the litany of values that can be learned from them. Both of my sons played sports in high school and college, and one, Larry, coaches football and track at a local high school. I am more than aware of the benefits that await the student athlete, and I know first hand what Larry teaches his kids.

I also see the influence of professional athletes on kids, and can't help but express alarm at the deterioration of sportsmanship over the past few decades, as high school athletes emulate the behavior and style of their heroes. Former basketball great Charles Barkley has it wrong when he says that professional athletes are not role models. "Parents, teachers, ministers, people like that, should be their role models," he asserts. Maybe so, but when Sir Charles punches out an opponent in an Olympic game, the kids who look up to him get the message it's all right, especially when Charles isn't punished for his actions. Ever seen a conductor body slam a pianist against his Steinway Grand because he missed a couple of notes? And symphony orchestras play incredibly well together, no single musician needing to shine, and with a total commitment to group achievement—teamwork at its highest level.

But the main reasons for exposing the next generation to the arts isn't about learning teamwork or having role models. It is about our culture, the most creative and beautiful aspects of humanity. It is about nurturing that side of us that nurtures.

The arts give us stability by linking us to our past and giving us the framework for measuring our evolution as a society, as much as science measures evolution of the development of various species of living things. The arts are also predictive of the future, as much or more than science. Scientists often are surprised by new developments, or simply describe events as unexplainable, when they appear to contradict accepted scientific theory, even law. Not so with the arts.

The science fiction of yesterday is the reality of today, as described Buck Rogers, who, in the nineteenth century, flew about in space with a baby rocket of sorts strapped to his torso, plus the writings of Jules Verne, Arthur C. Clarke, and others. Of course, Leonardo DaVinci drew pictures of submarines and helicopters. The dream, the art, came first. Science seized on the idea and made it a physical reality 500 years later.

To deprive our children from not going into the arts, and not encouraging them to participate in them has a more insidious negative repercussion. It channels their creativity elsewhere, which could have deleterious long term repercussions in the advancement of mankind through science. Do something about it.

Things Are A-Changin'

F or a while, it looked like Houston baseball fans were going to be saddled with their team playing its home games at Enron Field, because of a licensing agreement between the city and Enron. Fortunately, they worked it out. Licensing has spread throughout the sports world, well beyond the days when their owners named the Wrigley Fields, Bush Stadiums, Comisky Parks, and Griffith Stadiums of the world after themselves. At least those guys owned the teams, and it was their money.

Similar situations exist in the arts. Angels make significant donations to nonprofit organizations and have buildings named after them. In the Los Angeles Area, we have Royce Hall on the campus of UCLA, the Smothers Theater and Raitt Hall on the grounds of Pepperdine University, the Dorothy Chandler Pavilion, Mark Taper Forum, and so on. Without their generosity, there would be a significant void in the arts.

Other than the legacy of their names on those esteemed buildings, none of those Angels expected anything in return. They have no voice in what goes on inside. Neither John Raitt nor Tom Smothers demands that a friend get a gig at their house.

I am a season ticket holder for the Los Angeles Philharmonic and can hardly wait for my seats at Walt Disney Concert Hall, which will be the Philharmonic's new home in 2003. Disney will have no say in what the symphony plays, despite all their spending. Disney also made a sizable donation to the Smithsonian to help establish an Animation Museum within the Smithsonian's hallowed walls. Their animation is a major part of the permanent collection. Okay, Disney IS an important part of the history of animation, so I do not have a problem there. I am also okay, but a little uneasy, with the Smithsonian naming it "The Disney Museum." Disney brass agreed not to exercise any censorship—or pressure—as to what is exhibited there. I am worried more about a few years from now, as well as public perception.

But things, they are a-changin'. Museums are being strangled by budget cuts as the arts get a smaller slice of the Government pie. Politicians who tell you that fighting crime and providing better education, etc., must have a higher priority than art exhibits or fostering music programs, are a bit disingenuous. A case in point is New York, whose Department of Cultural Affairs shrank in half between 1990 and 2002, a time of economic growth. An additional 15 to 20 percent is likely under Mayor Michael Bloomberg's watchful eye in a tight economy. Before Bloomberg, Mayor Giuliani looked at the arts as economic development, applying the litmus test: how is art going to create in jobs and give back to the city?

So when the Giorgio Armani Company became an Angel to the Guggenheim Museum, to the tune of $15 million over a three-year period, one can understand why the museum launched a retrospective of the work of that Italian fashion designer eight months after the sponsorship agreement was signed. Corporations want something for their money. We live in a world of bean counters and answering to stockholders.

Just the appearance of an impropriety can be damaging. A few years ago, the board of the St. Louis Museum of Art declined a $50,000 exhibition-related gift from the Herman Miller Furniture Company. The donation was intended to help the museum hold the exhibition "The Work of Charles and Ray Eames." The museum declined the offer on the grounds that Herman Miller, which also helped finance the show itself, produces and markets Eames furniture. The board decided there might be an appearance of a conflict of interest if they accepted the money. The Miller people respected the decision, but regretted that they were not able to support more local activities in connection with the show.

Maybe there should be a place on front of the Form 1040 for taxpayers to donate $1 to $5 to an endowment for the arts, next to the box we can check to donate $3 to presidential campaigns. State tax forms could do the same.

It does not bode well for the future of a society that makes the arts expendable at the drop of a hat, or a budget.

Hey, that future includes my grandchildren! Here are my five bucks.

What He Saw Is
What We Got

*T*here are people who tell me to get off my soap box. Time to recognize that everything important is not about art. We live in the age of technology and scientific discovery and advancement, the era of rapid change and accelerated lives. The arts are important, I am told, but not the root of all that is good.

Okay. I admit I can get a bit overzealous. My passion for the arts is legendary, at least in the small circle in which I am known. I have been told that I am right to assert that art, in all its forms, enriches our lives, brings beauty and serenity to our planet. But that's about it, and to ascribe healing powers and scientific discovery to art is, well, just going to far. When I bring up such visionaries as H. G. Wells and Jules Verne, they are dismissed as science fiction writers, with an emphasis on 'fiction'.

I would like to share a story with you, about another favorite character of mine, "Little Leo." I mean, he could not have been over thirteen or fourteen, and he had played really hard, running and jumping [he became one of the greatest athletes of his time], so he curled up under a tree for an afternoon nap. He had the strangest dream. A bird appeared before him, right between his eyes, just opposite what some refer to as the 'middle eye' or mind's eye. It just hovered in front of him, its wings flapping so fast they were just about invisible and made a whirring sound. Leo opened his eyes and saw the same bird in front of him in the flesh. It was so close to him he could hear its wings whirling and could see a person inside the bird's eye. He did not realize it was his own reflection. After hovering a few moments, the 'whirlybird' flew away.

Leo was just as good an artist as he was an athlete, so he pulled out his sketch pad and drew the whirlybird. He drew it again and again, and, since the dream repeated itself over the next few years, he continued to draw it in squadrons, gradually making it less alive, more animated, larger versions with more people in them. And thus, the whirlybird was born, later to be called helicopters, when, nearly four hundred years later, science and technology caught up with the inventive mind of Leonardo Da Vinci.

Leonardo's visions brought us yet another twentieth century invention. He was busy swimming one afternoon, when he came eye-to-eye with a large fish. He noticed that the fish was carrying a passenger, a young man, clearly visible in its eye. It turned its head, to reveal another passenger visible in the other eye. Like in the case of the whirlybird, Leo was seeing reflections of himself. Still, with his fertile imagination, he sketched sleek black fish with people in them, guiding them, driving them. And thus, the submarine was born, as he gradually made them more and more mechanical over the years, predicting that the day would come when man would build mechanical fish which could be used beneath the sea. Again, Da Vinci was nearly four hundred years ahead of man's ability to build what he foresaw. There is no doubt, however, that he provided the blueprint for these important scientific discoveries and inventions. He provided similar ideas for laser beams and tanks. Writers like Wells and Verne advanced those ideas, bringing them closer to fruition with stories built around the inventions which began in Leonardo Da Vinci's head.

Call it science fiction. Emphasize the word fiction. But it is clear to me that the great visionary artists invariably predict the direction in which we move as a civilization. Art brings beauty to the world, while describing what is going on in the world, and it is the trigger that makes the fiction of today the reality of tomorrow.

To dismiss art as merely decorative or beautiful diminishes its value. Everything that is, starts as a thought. If something isn't imagined, it doesn't happen. We must encourage our children's participation in the arts. Let's not be so quick to stifle the arts in our schools, treating them as second-class citizens behind athletics. When we do, we reduce the discoveries which could emerge from the minds of artists. We all lose.

Ship of Fools

I have yet to have a column or story I wrote, "modified" for publication. No publisher or editor has felt the need to edit content. That does not mean that I have not received editorial advice, regarding rhetoric, or asked to tighten a story to fit a smaller space, but, ultimately, the decision was mine. Of course, if I failed to comply with a request, the decision to publish or not publish belongs to the publisher. On the other hand, I reserve the right to pull my column or story as well.

That is as it should be. There is a movement underway to alter works of art to comply with ethical standards established by a group of self-appointed arbiters of morality. They would say that they are protecting the rest of us from exposure to a litany of evils.

For example, Trilogy Studios, a Utah-based company invented and sells a software program known as "movie mask," which is used to sanitize R-rated movies. *Sanitize* is a euphemism for change, for censorship, done, I might add, without permission or license. *Sanitize* is another way of saying, "alter to make it fit into my notion of right or wrong." Did you see the blockbuster movie, *TITANIC*? In it, our hero, Leonardo DiCaprio is painting the beautiful Kate Winslet. She is naked, and we get some looks at her bare breasts, both on the couch and on the canvas. With "movie mask," we can cover her up. The head of Trilogy Studios, Breck Rose, says that they provide a choice to customers. We might as well clothe such masterpiece sculptures as Venus de Milo and David. Of course, if we send a picture of the Mona Lisa to a Muslim country, we should put a veil over her smile.

Blatant use of censorship is not limited to entrepreneurs like Mr. Rose. Well-intentioned educators are just as bad, even as they hide behind their cloak of innocence and the 'public good.' References to "Negroes"—even "niggers"—in the classic, *HUCKLEBERRY FINN*, have been removed. No matter that it was not only the language of the day, but Mark Twain beautifully showed the genuine affection between a runaway slave and a Southern white boy. Twain would be horrified by such censorship—he would probably turn over in his grave.

The short stories of Nobel Prize winner Isaac Bashevas Singer capture the Judaic heritage and Jewishness of the times. Judaism is more than an integral part of the stories. It is their reason d'etre.

Yet, in the same sweeping sanitization of great literature by no less than authorities representing the New York school system, all references to Jewish behavior had been removed on a high school regent exam. For example, Mr. Singer's reference to "Most Jewish Women" became "Most Women," and out entirely went the line, "Jews are Jews and Gentiles are Gentiles."

Other works by known authors had been equally sanitized. The State Education Department, which prepares the exams, said it had modified certain passages as it deemed appropriate, because "it did not want any student to feel ill at ease while taking the test." References to race, religion, ethnicity, sex, nudity, alcohol, even the mildest profanity, were excised from great literary works.

Ironically, students were required to answer questions based on the doctored versions. To compound that sin, the passages were marked as the works of the authors, without indicating that they had been modified. The outcry from authors was vehement and indignant. Frank Conroy, whose memoir, "Stop Time," was altered, the word "hell" replaced with "heck," and the elimination of all references to sex, religion, nudity and potential violence–all essential to an understanding of the passage, said: "I was just completely shocked. It's going through and taking out the flavor of the month." Annie Dillard, upon hearing about the removal of the racial content of one of her passages, wrote to the state: "What could be the purpose of an exercise testing students on such a lacerated passage . . . which finally, is neither mine nor true to my lived experience?" Other examples: a boy described as "skinny" became "thin," while another "fat" boy became "heavy." By the way, none of the authors were contacted prior to the emasculation of their masterpieces.

I have a suggestion: all those who would censor masterpieces, literally change them to suit their own politically correct but artistically blasphemous behavior, should have their own frame of reference. I hereby declare that all censors should be labeled *mentally handicapped*. By the way, I ran this column by a few friends before sending it to the publisher. The overwhelming favorite word describing those censors was *idiots*.

Art for Our Sake

"The world is too much with us.
Getting and spending, we lay waste our power."
William Wordsworth

*T*he great English poet began one of his most famous sonnets with those words more than two hundred years ago. Not much has changed, has it? We're still getting and spending, and we still lay waste our power.

Frankly, I admit that I enjoy the 'getting and spending' part. Especially the spending. It's the 'lay waste our power' that is the subject of this column. Invariably, when we waste our power, it translates into misdirecting our energies. And just as the squeaky wheel gets the oil, the loudest, biggest bang for the buck parts of our society get our attention.

In the sixties, the great management tool was cost versus benefit analysis. Put your money where you got the best return, not only in personal investment, but also in public expenditures. The name has changed, but the philosophy lingers on. The first programs to be slashed from the Federal budget are those with either [one] no constituency that could raise much of an outcry, or [two] not much of a monetary return. Guess what one of the first programs to go is. Support for the arts, under the name, National Endowment of the Arts.

It doesn't stop there. At state and local levels, art programs are the most expendable in schools. In grades 1-8, there is daily recess, sometimes twice daily. They might bring in an "art person" or a "music person" once a week. And then it gets worse. We place more emphasis on high school athletics than any other school activity. To make matters worse [better?], there must be equal opportunity for girls. In the name of equality among the genders, that means more money allocated to sports for extra coaches and equipment. What about the boy or girl who wants to paint? Or play the piano? Or simply hear classical music?

You probably don't care. Neither do other parents. If enough of you did, the outcry could become loud enough to cause a change.

As long as your daughter can play soccer or has a chance to play varsity softball, who cares about that other stuff? Maybe she'll win a scholarship and you won't have to pay her way through college. Ah, college. That's the ticket. If a child can't become a professional athlete and earn the really big bucks playing some game--and few do--they can learn a good job in college.

By the way, how many classical violinists have you known to be arrested for beating up another kid? Or mowing down fellow students with an Uzi? Classical pianists have strong hands and wrists. Hear of any strangling somebody? Did you hear about the artist who stabbed a fellow 12th grader over dessert in the cafeteria? Neither have I.

This is not to imply that people in the arts are morally superior to the rest of us. The gene of humanity's morals is remarkably consistent across color, gender, social status, national origin, and any other subset you care to examine.

A society that appreciates the arts and thus places greater emphasis on the creative spirit of mankind, tends to be a less aggressive society. It has also been proven that art therapy works. Both ways. By that I mean, people who engage in the arts show reduced signs of stress, lowering of their blood pressure and other physiological improvements. And people who simply look at, listen to, and enjoy the arts, are soothed by them, with comparable results. There are now degrees in Art Therapy offered at numerous colleges. What an outstanding opportunity for people who enjoyed showing their child's art when she was six, and became disillusioned when she wanted to be an artist. These days, making a living is more important than following one's passion or dream. It's the American Way. By the way, an artist, not a doctor or a lawyer, or a baseball player created that great poster of the American Flag in so many store windows.

There is an outcry in this country to get back to basic values. Let's make sure that, among those values, is an appreciation of beauty and tranquility. What good is a nation at peace, if its citizens find peace through Valium, Prosac, Zoloft, lithium—or harassing others?

Paradise Lost

*T*he tragedy of 9-11 has been lived and relived by all of us on a consistent if not daily basis since that Day of Infamy. It does not need to be rekindled, but I would like to weigh in from a somewhat different perspective. First and foremost, the citizens snatched away from their families and our society is the overwhelming loss. The Great Towers, which, it appears, will not be rebuilt to that grand scale, and the nearby buildings that suffered the same fate, represent a devastating loss at another level. The economic loss, immediate and through the ripple effect, could take years to recoup. The emotional and psychological impact that horrific event had on us, individually and as a society, changed our way of life forever.

The New York Times on the Web, about a week after the disaster, posted an article on another kind of loss, which I did not see get picked up anywhere else. A tragedy of another sort. A loss more reflective of the human potential than anything else. Still, we put numbers on everything, so here goes. Fifty million dollars worth of original art was lost. That number is not significant enough to make headlines in the scheme of things, and obviously was not worthy of mention on television. At least I never heard it, nor did any friends mention it to me.

There is much debate on what should be erected in place of the Towers. Buildings, a park, a memorial, and so forth. At last report, there were three proposals in the running, although the final result might well be a combination of them. Politicians lament the loss of revenue from office space rentals, and the ripple effect on the economy in downtown Manhattan. Other than the loss of lives, the focus is on money.

Did you ever see the mobile in the lobby of one of the Towers? A unique creation by America's first international artist, Alexander Calder. He is the Father of the mobile. You might remember the airplane painted to his creative specifications. The now defunct Braniff Airlines flew it, and it looked like an American Flag waving in the sky when it was in flight. My favorite mobile is the one in the atrium in the East Wing of the National Gallery of Art in Washington, D. C. Calder died in 1978. That means that the playful, beautiful, elegant, all-American mobile lost on 9-11 is lost forever. So what if it only cost a million or so bucks. The people who bought it thought it was well worth the money. It brought pleasure and prestige to their building. And it reflected the indomitable American spirit so elegantly reflected in the art of Alexander Calder. There was more. Paintings, tapestries, etchings, and sculptures by the likes of 20th century masters Picasso, Miro and Henry Moore, as well as important and emerging American artists died with the buildings. Jim Dine, James Rosenquist and some of the great Abstract Expressionists and Pop Artists created wonderful pieces that were proudly displayed not just in the lobbies of the lost buildings, but in corporate and private offices. Stellar representations of another aspect of the American Spirit and America's unique contribution to art. Lost forever.

Even when new buildings are erected, offices furnished and new art acquired and displayed, the "new" art does not replace the art that was destroyed. That is not to say that the replacement art will not be as aesthetically pleasing or as creatively inspired, either. But when original art is gone, it cannot be replaced, any more than hiring new employees replaces those lost souls.

As the anniversary of Nine Eleven is acknowledged, even as we mourn and glorify those who died, let us not forget the scope of our loss. Human life is not replaceable and the tragedy of its loss is overwhelming and incomprehensible. I am merely suggesting that the loss of the art is not to be dismissed. It's value is not as measurable as the economic loss suffered, but it counts.

I am confident that the corporations that move into the space eventually built will allocate a portion of their investment toward art. American corporations have, to a significant degree, become the art patrons of today. I would hope that those who represent the rest of us will recognize the value of art and insist on the inclusion of works of art in the public spaces.

Classical MTV in Your Home Town

K nowing today is a national holiday, when I woke up this morning, I immediately clicked on the television and Channel 26. I had a feeling my favorite show would be on. It was a touch before seven.

My instincts were right. Jorge Bolet was playing a ballade by Chopin. I smiled, propped up some pillows and relaxed for some early morning bliss. Patty had left me a thermos with coffee, so I poured a cup, just as Bolet finished and the next vignette was Errol Garner entertaining me with a mellifluous rendition of *Laura*, one of Garner's signature tunes on piano.

An animated film featuring a ballerina on a boat came next, filling me with joy with its lyricism, music and humor. The followup piece was a clip of three children from a dance academy in St. Petersburg, Russia, performing the pas de trois from Tchaikovsky's *Nutcracker Suite*, supported by music played by the Kirov Orchestra. Next came the incomparable Mahalia Jackson in her farewell concert at Royal Albert Hall in London, offering up two inspirational gospel songs, intertwined with Ms Jackson describing her attitude about life. Joan Sutherland performed an aria from Verdi's *La Traviata*. I was mesmerized by an excerpt from the 1927 classic silent film, *Uncle Tom's Cabin*, heard baritone, Bryn Terfel sing *Some Enchanted Evening*, followed by Kiri te Kanawa's rendition of *You'll Never Walk Alone*. Other favorites followed and I watched & dozed for the better part of two hours, until my telephone rang and I woke up to beautiful videography of the coast of France accompanied by DeBussey's *La Mer*, and finally an exciting dance piece by the Alvin Ailey Dance Theater.

My favorite show is not a show. It is a montage of videos spanning the arts. ALL the arts. It is the Classic Arts Showcase, a free cable television program designed to bring the classic arts experience to the largest audience possible by providing video clips of the arts in hopes that viewers will be tempted, in their words, "to go out and feast from the buffet of arts available in the community. Think of us as Classic MTV."

Classic Arts Showcase airs video samplings of animation, architectural art, ballet, chamber and choral music, dance, folk art, movies, museum art, musical theater, opera, orchestral, recital, solo instrumental, solo vocal, and theatrical performances, as well as classic film and archival documentaries. They are on the air 24-hours via satellite, covering most of North and South America.

I have often gone to bed with the TV on low, so if I wake up during the night I can be serenaded back to sleep by the likes of Caruso, Domingo, James Galway, Dizzy Gillespie, Thelonius Monk, or Yehudi Menuhin. WARNING: the showcase is habit-forming, and I find myself sitting up in bed at 4:00 A.M., unwilling to turn the set off, for fear of missing a Buster Keaton vignette, or perhaps Lillian Gish, or Arturo Toscanini conducting the NBC symphony orchestra, Rudolph Valentino playing the sheik, or some other classic I will treasure. I once awoke to the inimitable sound of a Chopin scherzo played by Sviatoslav Richter. I have thirty CD's of Richter playing piano, and had never seen him perform. Since the showcase is an eight-hour collection of clips that is repeated, I timed it so I saw my hero on the piano perform that scherzo three times in a twenty-four period. Thank you, Classic Arts Showcase.

They don't sell the videos, although, on their website, www.classicartsshowcase.org, they provide a list of all their sources. They also do not accept donations. They are one hundred percent funded by the Lloyd E. Rigler-Lawrence E. Deutsch Foundation.

They provide a public service that touches my heart as it touches the soul of our society. If you do not get them in your area, call your local cable company and ask them to carry the Classic Arts Showcase. It won't cost them a dime and they owe it to their subscribers. I especially think it is important for our children. I can't say it better than they do on their web site:

"As a major arts supporter our Foundation has long known how important music and the arts can be in a child's life. The arts encourage self-esteem, develop strong bodies and critical thinking, and even help math scores. As you know, arts education is hard to find in public schools. And recent studies by the National Endowment for the Arts and The President's Committee on the Arts and Humanities show that, despite higher incomes and better levels of education younger Americans are unlikely ever to attend live performances of 'highbrow' culture, especially classical music, opera and musical and dramatic theater. Our kids desperately need to be exposed to the arts. That is the purpose of our Foundation supported satellite arts program, Class Arts Showcase, offered free and unscrambled as a public service to the United States."

'Nuff said.

The Business of Art

*T*hese columns focus on issues related to business aspects of art, providing guidelines every art buyer & seller should know, as well as the pitfalls and dangers in buying and selling art.

Are You Kidding, Sotheby's?

*D*id you hear about the sale of the Andy Warhol painting of Marilyn Monroe at Sotheby's? The pre-auction estimate [Sotheby's best estimate of a fair price for both buyer and seller] was $4.5 million. Two anonymous bidders went at it by telephone like Ninja warriors as a startled, then mesmerized group of people sat live at the auction and listened with disbelief and amazement as the bidding zoomed past the $5 million mark, then ten, and shot by fifteen, to a record $17.3 million. In the words of Carl Vowel of the New York Times [3/15/98 edition], "when it ended, the packed salesroom burst into thunderous applause." The painting isn't exactly a painting. It is a hand colored photograph and serigraph, from a series of silk-screen portraits that Warhol created in 1964.

The after sale comments of Mr. Tobias Meyer, Director of Sotheby's Department of Contemporary Art-Worldwide, were equally remarkable. First, he complimented both bidders and especially the buyer on how good a deal the buyer made. In Mr. Meyer's words, "The Warhol is a wise buy at this price." Then he added, "It will soon be worth as much as Picasso or any landmark work of this century." Smart thinking. At least smart talking. If I sold a client a work of art for four times what I thought it would sell for and thought was a fair price, I would reassure him, too. If Mr. Meyer thought the piece was a good buy at $17.3 million, why would his department's fair price estimate be one-fourth of that? And how does he know that it will soon be worth four times the $17.3 million, which is the implication of his remark that compared the piece to Picasso and other landmark works? I prefer influential people to exercise restraint and err on the side of caution.

Since the Warhol is a silkscreen print, I will describe original printmaking most widely used by artists.

First, an original print is NOT a reproduction. Color reproductions are produced by combining four negatives that are manipulated to produce every color. You can distinguish reproductions from hand made prints, using a jeweler's loop, and looking for rows of dots that compose these separations. An original print does not have dots.

Reproductions have no investment value, as editions can be unlimited. Original prints are works of art, as original as paintings, and have been made by many masters and today's leading artists. The artist creates images on stones, plates or screens—a separate one for each color. This can take months. Each print is rolled by hand through a press or under a stencil, again, a separate pull for each color. The artist rejects any imperfect prints, because they can't print over them the way they can paint over a painting. Popular acknowledged techniques are:

LITHOGRAPHY. Based on the concept that oil and water don't mix, the artist draws directly onto stones with an oily crayon, and ink is transferred to paper via a high- powered litho press. Up to 20 stones can be used to produce a colorful lithograph. Chagall and Miro were fond of original lithography.

ETCHING. Gets its name from either the Dutch [etsen] or German [atsen], meaning to eat. The artist draws on specially treated plates that are immersed in acid baths, and the acid bites into the plate, creating grooves, which hold the ink when the artist applies it to the plate. The plate is put under great pressure, and the inks are pressed out of the furrows onto the paper. Rembrandt, Goya and Picasso used the etching technique extensively and with great success.

SERIGRAPHY. The artist makes stencils of screens of silk mesh, and ink is pressed through open areas onto the paper. There can be more than 50 screens used to produce one image. Serigraphy became popular in the 1960's, when Andy Warhol, Jasper Johns, Leroy Neiman and others adopted it, because of its ability to produce bright areas of color.

Original prints are an outstanding way to collect art, because they are more affordable prices than unique paintings by the masters. Whereas a Picasso painting sells in the tens of millions, his original etchings sell in the thousands.

Don't Buy Art at a Yard Sale!

P eople like to brag about the piece of art they bought at a fraction of its value. Maybe they spied it lying on the ground at a yard sale. Everybody likes a bargain. Including me. If you can get me a BMW for the price of a KIA, I'll be at your house in twenty minutes. Of course, I will insist that you allow me lift up the hood with the BMW emblem on it, and check out the engine. You also couldn't blame me if I wanted to start it up and drive it, to see if it accelerates and corners like a BMW or a KIA.

The new millennium yard sale may well be eBay, the cyber-garage store of the Internet—the new haven for bargains, and I don't mean that wonderful town in Connecticut. I am not here to impugn eBay. They are not doing anything legally wrong. Morally might be another issue. But PLEASE! Be careful what original art you "steal" on line. After spending the past hour scrolling through art works being auctioned on eBay, I am compelled to warn you. I found many of the listed items misleading, if not downright misrepresentations of what they are.

A signed Picasso linocut for $160? I don't think so. First of all, there are no original linocuts by Picasso as small as 8X10 inches. Second, his linocuts sell in the thousands, often over $50,000. An "original" lithograph from the Vollard Suite for $95? No such animal. The Vollard Suite consists of one hundred *etchings*. The lithographs are reproductions of those etchings, hardly original. Not unlike photocopies on really good paper, and beautifully packaged and boxed. That doesn't mean you shouldn't buy one, if you like it. Just don't pay five times what it's worth, because you think it is something it isn't. And there was that signed and numbered lithograph by Marc Chagall. Except that it was not an original lithograph and Chagall had nothing to do with it. Years after his death, some people reproduced a limited number of copies of a Chagall painting. These are offset lithographs, reproductions, like the cover of TIME Magazine, photo-mechanically reproduced, not an original anything. The seller revealed that the signature was a facsimile. That means that a stamp was made of Chagall's signature and applied to the reproduction.

Etchings by Rembrandt turned out to be not by Rembrandt. Ditto for etchings by Renoir. I found that the works attributed to the Masters were often mislabeled, descriptions of them misleading, and references about them specious. It is especially offensive when the offerings are by art dealers who you think would know better. Makes one wonder if they really are art dealers.

Some people I have known in the art world for years are selling online, and they honestly describe exactly what they are—and are not—offering. Unfortunately, [one] you might not know who they are, and [two] you might not know who they are not--so bidding online for novices is challenging work.

Not all the works by masters are misrepresented. Amongst the rubble were some gems: an aquatint by Picasso from the 347 series—catalogued and & correctly described; an authentic Picasso ceramic plate, also accurately described and referenced to the appropriate catalog. With my 27 years experience in the art world, specializing in the 20th century masters, I can cull the good from the bad and the ugly. I suspect that the average person has no idea what they are buying online.

Unless you are an experienced art buyer, and know the real meaning of such terms as lithograph, etching, signed & numbered, original, print, et al, don't bid on anything that costs more than you are willing to lose. Remember, if something appears too good to be true, it probably is. Tell the truth. If you were driving by a yard sale, where a family was moving and getting rid of stuff it no longer needed or wanted, and you saw this piece of art in a nice frame, and you could read the signature, *"Picasso,"* and the man told you that it's been in his family for years, and he wanted ten dollars for it, even though he "knew" it was an original signed Picasso, would you believe him?

Happy hunting.

Don't Get Trapped in the Net

I recently made myself available on-line at one of those web sites where people can ask questions on a seemingly endless range of subjects. No, I do not answer personal questions. My purpose is to spread the word about art and provide interested parties with information useful for collecting and enjoying art.

I am telling you this not to get you to write to me at that website. You don't need to go through that. I am always available to my readers through this newspaper or magazine [depending where you are reading this] or at my email address at the end of the column.

There are literally dozens of web sites to choose from, and there is no screening process by which the site providers select their "experts." Wanna be an expert? Tell them you are, give 'em your "credentials" and you are part of the team. I decided to do some investigative reporting. Here are some of my findings.

On person declared himself an art expert, using this justification: I paint watercolors and appreciate beautiful art. I have also taken a course in art history. Another announced that he owned art by Dali and Picasso. And these guys are disseminating information about collecting art, offering opinions about investing in art, various techniques and mediums, and answering questions from people relying on their expertise before investing in art.

Most of the questions solicit opinions about particular art, or where to find information, so the answers are harmless enough: *"Go to such and such web site and type in the artist's name,* or, *"I prefer so and so, because..."* No one is going to get hurt by that.

Unfortunately, not all the answers are benign. When an "expert" talks about works of art as "paintings" and "lithographs" and "etchings" regarding a suite of original *wood block prints*, he is misleading the public. And then he had the audacity to ask for pictures of the art, so he could give an appraisal. Free, of course. How can he appraise something when he does not even know what it is? Some unsuspecting person is relying on the "expert" for advice which could affect whether he buys and what he pays for a piece of art.

I could fill this and a few more columns with other equally bothersome examples. The above example is not isolated. And the problem is exacerbated by the number of people using the net for information. The web sites I visited had handled a total of more than a thousand questions about art in less than a two week period.

Several friends have referred me to the net for information in areas I expressed an interest. If the "experts" I go to are as reckless, if not downright ignorant about their so-called area of expertise, how do I know I can rely on the information I get? The truth is: I CAN'T.

Students browse the internet, too. At least one out of every five questions in the fine art category were from people seeking information for school papers or other projects, from the high school to college levels. Although I occasionally answer a question or voice an opinion, more often than not, I refer them to sources found in brick and mortar. I encourage them to do their own homework.

Call me old-fashioned, but there is nothing better than research in libraries, or in the case of fine art, visiting museums, seeing art first hand, or perusing the array of quality art books by recognized authorities.

Of course, relying on something in print is no guarantee, either. The difference is, the author generally offers up his or her credentials. For some reason, I have found less people ready to proclaim themselves as experts because they own something or read a book about it. There seems to be something insidious about the internet that emboldens people to do that.

Have you seen crazy, irresponsible drivers on the road who display extremely poor judgment and wondered how they got their driver's license? Certainly, the enormous traffic thundering down the information highway raises the same question. Just be careful. Terms like inter*net* and *web* site may be warnings. Don't get trapped in the net.

Buy Art for the Right Reasons

*M*y cousin Frank has a standard procedure when he sees me. The last time was on a cruise ship embarking from Barcelona, Spain. I had just been introduced as the art director & auctioneer for the cruise, and when the intros where done, Frank came running up to me with outstretched arms, flung himself around me, and bellowed without a breath, "Hey cuz, fancy meeting you here. This is great. Darlene and I are taking our first cruise, from here to Venice and back. And hey, what are the Agams and Dalis worth that I bought from you?"

Now Frank doesn't care what they are worth. He has absolutely no intention of selling them. I once told him he could get nearly three times what he paid and when could I come by and get them. He withdrew like a moth when you turn out the light. He bought them because he and Darlene liked them. He just enjoys hearing how much they have gone up in value, and enjoys just as much others hearing what a smart decision he made.

Most people buy art to beautify their homes or decorate their offices. Others enjoy the prestige of having works by 20th century masters and other famous artists that they can show their family and friends. Frank's scene with me accomplished it all. Very few people actually sell art that they love.

But things, they may be a-changin'. I belong to an Art Service based in Paris, which provides prices for art sold at auction around the world. They have been an invaluable resource for appraisals and simply seeing who is hot and who is not. They recently expanded their services. They have established an econometrics department and offer quantitative information and analysis regarding the art market. They have provided data to such international media organizations as CNN and Business Week. They are supporting those who would sell art as an investment.

Not that it isn't. According to their numbers, since 1996, the painting segment of the art market has provided an average annual return of nearly seven percent. They note that nearly 90 percent of artworks sell for less than EUR10,000 at auction, and many original graphics sell for substantially less, making art accessible to more than just the wealthy, dispelling a long-time myth about who can afford art.

I am not surprised. Art attracts art lovers as well as investors, who buy art for the aesthetic pleasure as much as for investment. But what is the "right" art for investing? Not necessarily the popular art of the day. It is the art of the masters, which transcends tastes and trends. Art that endures over time, so there is always a demand for it. At the same time, the inelastic supply puts pressure on its price. For example, with less Picasso works available than a decade ago, and nothing new coming from the grave, increased demand means higher prices.

That is well and good, and investors who have soured with the decline in the stock market might benefit financially by putting part of their investment portfolio in art. But knowing what to buy is no different than knowing what stocks to buy, and picking an art dealer or gallery is as tricky as selecting a stockbroker.

A few tips: [1] only buy "name brands," artists with great reputations over long periods of time [you might miss a few winners, but the likelihood of being stuck with something you can't sell is greatly reduced]; [2] select an art dealer you are comfortable with, the same as you would an accountant, financial advisor, doctor, or lawyer; [3] don't pay retail. I know my friends in the art gallery business will be unhappy with me saying that, but the difference between retail and wholesale can be substantial, and there can be years of appreciation required just to break even. Finally, do what I do: [4] buy what you love, hang it on your wall and enjoy it. Face it, there is a chance it will never go up in value, or, if it does, you might not need the money, opting instead for enjoying it and ultimately passing it on to your family.

My cousin Frank has the right idea!

Ask the Art Maven™

F irst of all, what the heck is a *maven*? I heard the word quite a lot growing up. It came out of Yiddish, and, in the Jewish community, it referred to someone who knew a lot about a particular topic. "Want to know about the best Canadian whiskey? Ask Uncle Irv. He's a whiskey maven!" How about furniture. "Ask Uncle Goodie, the furniture maven." The rest of the family always asked my dad about cooking. Dad was a food & cooking maven. He also happened to be a maven on religious matters.

The term has crept into the every day vernacular of English in the country. I have even heard it used on television, to describe experts in such fields as stocks & bonds, movies, military affairs, legal matters, and technology. The term has achieved sufficient stature to be included in the *ENCARTA WORLD ENGLISH DICTIONARY*. The North American Edition defines "maven" as:

"**expert or enthusiast:** somebody who is an expert or knowledgeable enthusiast in a particular field. Mid 20th Century. Via Yiddish "meyvn" from Hebrew literally "somebody who understands."

Rarely is a maven a self-appointed expert. It is more of an honorary title bestowed upon someone who displays expertise in a particular field, someone sought after when an explanation or understanding about a topic is required. For a long time, the media besieged ex-Secretary of State Henry Kissinger for his opinion on important world issues. His expertise lent credibility to the news. He was the maven on international affairs, before the term had widespread acceptance. A television interviewer bestowed the title *art maven* on me in the mid-nineties. I appreciated it and have hung onto it. It is even an integral part of my personal email address.

At the end of every *Art Beat* column is an invitation to my readers to submit questions and comments about the column and art. From time to time, I include the question or the subject matter in future columns. My selection criteria are based on [one] potential reader interest, [two] most frequently asked questions, [three] an opportunity for me to give readers important information that could help them with their collecting & investing, to appreciating & enjoying fine art, and, finally, [four] political and social issues regarding the arts.

The past year or so, I have volunteered my services to a few web sites that provide people the opportunity to ask questions of "experts" in various fields. Although I fancy myself as a gourmet cook and theater aficionado, I limit myself to questions on art.

Rather than print columns that would not otherwise be selected for inclusion in this collection, I have sifted through questions I have received and selected those that I believe will be of the greatest interest or value to you. Some overlap but they represent the greatest concern of readers or are of sufficient value that they are worth reading, despite some redundancy. A few general questions of a more esoteric nature have been included, because they afford me the opportunity to climb aboard my soap box and expound on subjects dear to me. Excuse the self-indulgence.

Ask the Art Maven™

*Everything You Always Wanted to Know About Art
and Didn't Know Who to Ask*

Question: Which type of art appreciates the most in monetary value?

Answer: "Type" can have several meanings. Do you mean historically, such as old masters versus modern masters, or by school, such as Impressionist versus Abstract Expressionist? Or, perhaps, by medium, such as painting versus sculpture? Then there is the question of unique versus original prints, famous names versus unknowns. If you were to buy art for investment, your safest bet would be a "brand name." By that, I mean famous artists with historical significance, whose art has a better chance of appreciating in value, because the demand for it continues even after they die, while supply obviously does not. Liquidity is also better, since works by masters tend to have international markets. Buying art by unknown, emerging, regional, or popular artists of the day, no matter how talented or popular, is risky. There is no assurance that there will be demand for the work in the future, as taste and popularity in the arts changes. If there is no demand or no one pushing the art, to whom do you sell?

Works by unknowns can increase in value. You could also win the Lottery or dig for and strike oil on your front lawn. If you like the work of an artist, famous or not, THAT is the reason to buy it. Enjoying art is reason enough. Much of the art in my personal collection has appreciated in value, but I cannot envision parting with any of it.

Question: I have been offered a lithograph from the Vollard Suite by Picasso. Is that a good investment?

Answer: Beware! The Vollard Suite is one of Picasso's tours de forces, a suite of 100 ETCHINGS he created in the 1930's for his friend and dealer, Ambrose Vollard. Each piece was pulled in an edition of 200, signed by Picasso in pencil, and is listed in the Bloch Catalog of Picasso Etchings. The lithographs were reproduced well after Picasso died. They are reproductions created by offset lithography in the same size and format as the originals, and beautifully packaged. If you like the image and can buy it for less than a hundred dollars, go ahead. The original Vollard etchings sell from $6,000 to $20,000, depending on the image and condition. The lithographic reproduction, although nice to look at, will never be worth more than you paid.

Question: How do I find out if a painting is of value and if the artist is still selling?

Answer: You have asked two of the most frequently asked questions I have gotten in my nearly three decades in the art world. Unfortunately, there are many talented artists who have sold works but never achieved fame or a consistent market. If you know where an artist lives—or lived—you can call galleries in that area. Many artists become big fish in small ponds and are regionally known. Beyond that, you can try the name on the web and search. A growing number of artists have web sites, or their works are shown at galleries who list them on their web sites. As for value of a specific work, if you can't find a marketplace, the bad news is that it is worth whatever you can sell it for, or, what someone is willing to pay. Enjoy the art and it is worth whatever you paid for it and more.

Question: What are the most expensive works by American artists?

Answer: According to auction records for the past fifteen years, the winner is George Bellows at $27,702,500. A fairly distant second is Willem De Kooning at $20,690,000, followed by

Andy Warhol at $17,327,500. The ten million dollar mark has been passed eleven times, including three times each by de Kooning [all in the top six] and Mark Rothko. Jasper Johns, Jackson Pollock and John Singer Sargent are the others in that elite group. The top woman is Georgia O'Keeffe, whose $6,166,000 sale ranked 27th. She had two others in the top 100. Mary Cassatt had a $4 million piece which came in 66th, the only other work by a woman to make the list.

Question: Please tell me how to evaluate the arts.

Answer: Who is to say what is good or bad? As the Bard said through Hamlet, "things are neither good nor bad, but thinking makes them so." Trust your instincts. Whatever the art form, painting, writing, music, you know what you like and what you don't. Do not let anyone tell you that you are wrong. On the other hand, if there is a piece of art you "don't get," give it a chance. Remember, as a kid you probably didn't like broccoli or asparagus. Maybe you still don't, but experimenting is how your tastes broaden.

Question: I just purchased a large nude oil on canvas, signed by the artist, "A. Ritter." I've looked on the web and cannot find anything about this artist and now I wonder if I spent too much. Do you have any information about this person?

Answer: I have not heard of the artist, A. Ritter. However, that isn't relevant. Most of the art that people buy is by an artist that no else has heard of, simply because there are so many artists out there. Unless you buy a household name, that is not important. Something made you buy the art. I assume that something is that you liked it, were drawn to it, related to it, felt a connection to it. Only you know if you paid too much, because only you know how much pleasure you get from it. What it boils down to is, beauty really is in the eye of the beholder.

Question: I recently purchased a Rembrandt print on canvas, titled "Saskia." It says on the back No. 426, Printed in the USA. I also purchased "Jeune Dame de Montmarte" by Modigliani, produced by the same company. Can you tell me if they have any value?

Answer: The masters did not print on canvas. There wasn't even a USA when Rembrandt did his etchings. These pieces are photo reproductions printed in virtually unlimited editions. Their value is the same as a reprint or poster, a few dollars.

Question: I'm a reporter for Popular Science Magazine, and I was wondering if you had any thoughts on a recent art-related question posed by a reader. First, why do the eyes in certain paintings and portraits seem to follow you around the room? Second, how do artists achieve this trick of the eye?

Answer: As an art lover, I am going to offer a very unscientific thesis to your question. I just completed a test, using my local newspaper. I looked through it for photographs of people. Those looking DIRECTLY into the camera, the equivalent of looking directly at me or you, well, when I moved my head, their eyes and mine remain locked. Not so for the others. So perhaps the "trick" is to paint the subject as though she is looking right at you. Try it out. If you learn a more scientific answer, please let me know. [*NOTE: Brad Dunn used my answer, giving me appropriate credit, in the June 2002 edition of Popular Science. Thank you, sir.*]

Question: We have an original etching by Salvador Dali titled "El Cid," with a certification by the New York Collectors Guild. What is the piece worth today?

Answer: El Cid is a charming etching by Dali. It was done in numerous editions, including black, brown, sepia, at least one pencil signed edition—maybe a few. There are also editions signed in the plated. So there are literally thousands of El Cid pieces in the world. That prevents it from being worth much, despite its artistic charm. It is probably worth a hundred dollars. I have sold them in charity auctions in the $70-$150 range in the past few years. Glad you like it, though. So do I.

Question: I was recently given an etching titled "Pour Roby," which appears to be authentic. It looks very much like all of the other etchings that I have seen online, except that the name of the painting and the signature are backwards. Is this in fact a rare piece or is it not genuine? And what is it worth?

Answer: "Pour Roby" is an original etching by Picasso. The title and his name are backwards on the paper, because Picasso scratched them into the etching plate. When the plate was inked and paper put on it and an image pressed onto it, voila, it comes out backwards—a mirror image. Although it is a real etching, it is from an open plate, i.e., over runs and restrikes. There are thousands of them out there. The retail value is less than two hundred dollars. It is nice, though, so enjoy it.

Question: I recently purchased a lovely oil on board signed "Hundman." I would like to know how to research this or any "fine arts artist."

Answer: I wish there was a secret formula I could share with you on researching artists. Who is to say what or whom that notion includes? I belong to an international service that has compiled auction results for more than 270,000 artists from the 4th century to the present. Millions of entries. No "Hundman" anywhere. There is no way to find him/her unless you know what region of the country, if the country is, in fact, USA. Then you could call local galleries. Unfortunately, many fine artists become well established in their area, and produce excellent art, and nothing else becomes of them, due to lack of promotion, bad marketing, bad luck, or changing tastes. You obviously respect and enjoy the art. Let that be enough. Art for Art's Sake is always reason enough.

Question: **Should creative practitioners balance or prioritize aesthetic and social issues? Also, any reference material and arts that would be great examples?**

Answer: Are you curious or doing a school project? Creative practitioners [artists] owe nothing to anyone in their art. Different artists are driven by different motives, and can have different purposes among their works. Many artists include social issues as their motivation—Picasso's "Guernica" is a passionate view of the horrors of war, for example. That's an easy one. Is "The Last Supper" a social issue? How about the works of Matisse? Music can be simply beautiful, or have a message, like Beethoven's 9th symphony, which begs for world unity and peace, and there are the songs of today's rappers. What is right? Literature abounds with social commentary, of course. Make a list of major works in visual art, music, and writing, and draw your own conclusions. Most of the time, the answer to your question will be obvious.

Question: Does art teach us anything? Can we look at art as an educator? If not, shall we consider it as an object of entertainment only?

Answer: The question seems more appropriate for a discussion group or the topic of a column, but I'll allow myself to do a stream of consciousness. First, consider this—according to zen masters, even a stone can be a teacher. So why not art? Art can provide futuristic messages in all the art forms [but doesn't have to]. For example, Jules Verne, Buck Rogers, Isaac Asimov, Arthur Clarke, Ray Bradbury, and George Orwell are writers who anticipated the future. Yesterday's science fiction is often today's reality. Visual artists have been equally futuristic in their art, beginning with Leonardo Da Vinci, whose pictures of laser beams, submarines and helicopters inspired the future, waiting only for technology to catch up with his vision. Artists are often visionaries, so art can give us an idea as to where we are headed as a society, as a civilization. One of my concerns is that today's visionary art views the future world as technological, devoid of art. I hope they're wrong, but suspect they're not.

Art can also mirror who, what and where we are as a society, depicting current situations through literature, painting and music. Today's music, like it or not, accurately describes a part of our society. Picasso's "Guernica" shows the hell of war. Shakespeare described the human condition. And so on. Just as the Museum of Natural History and the National Aeronautical and Space Museum chronicle man's trek in those directions, other great museums of the world house works of art that provide a pictorial history of mankind. Or, if you prefer, you look at pretty pictures as objects of entertainment only. It's up to you.

Question: I have a mint condition book by Andrew Wyeth. The title is "Pictures of Helga," or something similar. How much is it worth? I have some other art books, too.

Answer: Unless the book by Wyeth contains original prints, such as hand-pulled lithographs, etchings or wood block prints, the value is no more than the face or published price, unless it is a rare and sought after book. I would doubt this book fits that category. Art books do not traditionally appreciate in value. Collect them, as I do, for the beauty contained in them. When I buy an old book, used or new, I rarely pay anywhere near the original published price. I also collect first edition books by authors I enjoy, and when signed by the author, if she is famous, or if the books become classics and are out of print, they can appreciate. A true story: in 1988 I did a book signing in Scottsdale, AZ, and when I dedicated and signed a copy of my book to a reader/fan, she asked me what I thought it was worth. My answer: "I don't know. How much does a defaced book go down in value?"

Question: Where and when does postmodernism begin? What are the typical features of artists in this movement?

Answer: Modern art covers the gamut from surrealism and

cubism through abstract expressionism and pop art. After they stopped being examined, explored, advanced, even mimicked by artists, by definition, that was it. So whatever comes after modern art is post-modern. It had no definable or recognizable style. It is an amorphous conglomeration, if you will, of previous movements, a crazy quilt of conflicting styles and qualities. In my judgment, many of the "experimental" artists today, in all the artistic mediums, are searching for something different, searching for themselves, under the guise of "doing their own thing." They seem to be waiting to be discovered as the new school or movement leader.

Question: I own two Chagall lithographs, neither of which is signed. One is numbered & has Chagall's signature printed with a lithograph or wood block facsimile. The other is neither numbered nor signed. It is the "Ville de Nice" and was printed by "Ch. Sorlier Grav." I fear that an expert appraisal would cost more than the value of the prints since they were almost certainly printed after Chagall's death. What do you think?

Answer: Your intuition is correct. The two pieces are not particularly valuable. The one with the facsimile signature is from a series of images often sold at art auctions on cruise ships and low-end galleries. The signature is a stamp. It is a lithograph of a painting done by Chagall, produced well after his death. It sells in the $300-700 range. The unsigned piece is a different story. Charles Sorlier was Chagall's assistant and closest friend for more than sixty years. He helped Chagall with the creation of stones, even drew some himself from Chagall paintings. Sorlier did not have a printing company. The print is probably an offset lithograph [reproduction using 4-color process]. Look at it through a jeweler's loop or magnifying glass. Rows of dots are the telltale sign of an offset. Its value would be in the $30 range. If there are no dots, the print is from lithographic stones and its value would be in the $200 range.

Question: What is the difference between an etching and a lithograph?

Answer: An etching is an original work of art created by the artist drawing on specially treated plates that are then immersed in acid baths. The acid bites [eats!] into the plate, creating grooves that hold the ink when the artist applies it to the plate. The plate is put under great pressure, and the inks are pressed out of the furrows onto the paper, which has been moistened to prevent cracking under the pressure. The process gets its name from either the Dutch [etsen] or German [atsen], which means to eat.

Lithography is based on the concept that oil and water don't mix. For an original lithograph, the artist draws directly on stones with an oily crayon, the stone is wet, and oil-based ink is applied, adhering to the crayon. The ink is transferred to paper via a high-powered press. Up to 20 stones can be used to produce a colorful lithograph. An original lithograph is not to be confused with offset lithographs, which are reproductions created from photographs and the 4-color separation process.

Question: I found this item on ebay and was wondering if you could please take a peek and give me your opinion as to its authenticity. I am skeptical myself. [Ed. note: it was a Magritte "pencil drawing"]

Answer: I would not give my opinion as to the authenticity of the piece. I do know that being able to buy a Magritte pencil drawing for $450 is like buying a Rolls Royce for the price of a Honda. Make that a Honda motor scooter. I love Magritte but will not bid on the piece. Perhaps you could ask the seller what kind of provenance he or she has.

Question: I have a male bulldog made entirely of papier-mache'. He stands 14 inches on four paws and is 29 inches long, painted in oils and very life like. His teeth are showing. The name of the artist is hard to read as some paint is missing. This was given to my grandmother in 1932 by a priest at St.

Ignatius Church in Buchanan Valley Adams County, PA. Any information about the artist, date and value would be greatly appreciated.

Answer: Sorry, I cannot help you on the bulldog and don't even know where to send you. However, he sounds terrific. Why not name him and enjoy him. That would make him priceless.

Question: I recently came across a crossword. An art expert should be able to recognize a___ [fill in the blank] picture. A fine or a fake?

Answer: Shouldn't an expert be able to recognize both a fine and a fake picture? However, since "fine" could be in the eye of the beholder, a matter of opinion, my answer would be "fake."

Question: My wife and I have begun to purchase paintings of contemporary realist arts from what we believe is a reputable gallery. We primarily bought these paintings because we liked them. We are unsure whether we paid fair market price for these works or overpaid. They offered us a 10% discount but I don't know if we could have bargained for more. How can we determine what paintings are worth? Also, how good an investment are realist paintings in general as well as relative to other types of artwork?

Answer: Paintings don't come from manufacturers or artists with stickers on them showing suggested retail price. That could be true for limited edition works from certain publishers. Of course, when buying a new car, which has a sticker on it, how do you know how well you do, unless you go to the trouble of determining true dealer cost, with hold backs, etc.? And we are all not equal negotiators. In all likelihood, galleries pay half of the retail for graphic editions, although owners, too, have different negotiating skills, so some could get more, especially if they sold more. Discounts to galleries on unique and expensive works are usually less. The discounts galleries offer are also determined by their location and overhead, as well as your negotiating skill.

Other considerations: Can you find other galleries carrying the same artists? Can you locate the artists themselves and find out fair market value based on their sales? If not, DO NOT buy art because you "primarily" like it. That must be 100% of the reason. You must love it. DO NOT treat art as an investment commodity. Unless you buy a "name brand" [international reputation over years], the likelihood of the art appreciating AND your being able to sell for a profit are very unlikely.

Realist paintings are worth no more or less than other "schools" of art. It is about the artist. And, to be redundant, unless you are buying art by a household name, make sure you love it.

Question: How successful are commercial galleries? What counts as a commercial gallery? Nowadays many cafes, etc. sell art on the side. Would they fit in under the title? Is only modern art displayed in these galleries? I would be very grateful if you could answer any of my queries.

Answer: The fact that you "would be very grateful" if I gave you my take on galleries and your related questions makes me wonder as to your underlying purpose. Nothing devious, mind you, but it could help me answer you. Sounds like more than idle curiosity. Interested in opening a gallery or investing in one? Or selling art to them? There are many successful commercial galleries throughout the U. S. and Europe. In Japan, major department stores have long been a major gallery substitute. Ebay and other internet venues have cut into gallery sales. Regarding art at cafes and whether or not that makes them galleries: if they have fashion shows, would you consider them dress shops? Modern versus traditional: equal amounts of each.

The disadvantage of a commercial gallery: high overhead and full retain price to the collector. The advantage: visibility and often education to the collector who doesn't know anything about art. What is a commercial gallery? A retail space devoted PRIMARILY to the exhibit and sale of original art works.

Question: I have an original etching, an artist proof, from the 1930's, signed on the back by Ronald, on the front, by L. Ronald. I can't find any information on the artist. Maybe he was well known in his day, but since has taken a critical nosedive. Can you help?

Answer: Sorry, but the artist does not appear on my radar screen. I have numerous works by artists in the same situation, i.e., that no one knows. Fortunately, I like the art, and that is all that matters. Like others in the arts—singers, authors, other artists—only a handful make it from generation to generation.

Question: I own a picture by Bierstadt. It has the artist's last name in the lower right corner. On the back it reads: #725 Bierstand-18x24, "Island in the Sound," made in Holland. It appears to be paper on cardboard. Is it a painting or a print? Can you tell me what to look for to tell if it is a painting?

Answer: You do not have a painting. There would be one in the world and would not have number on the back, or where it was printed. It is likely a reproduction. Look at it through a jeweler's loop or high powered magnifying glass, and you should see rows of dots, indicating the 4-color separation process used to print reproductions via offset lithography.

Question: I would like to show my paintings. My family thinks I am a good artist. How and where do I start?

Answer: The next time you show your art to a family member or friend and they tell you how good it is, offer to sell it to them for a nominal amount, say $20. Never give it away. Go to local art fairs and festivals and talk to other artists. Perhaps rent a booth and display your work. Even if you don't sell anything, feedback from strangers is a lot more constructive and instructive than from family and friends. After showing at local events, make appointments and visit local galleries, who, if they like your work, will probably want it on consignment rather than buying an untested artist. Do not take rejection personally. I have had far more rejections than publishing of my writing. It is the nature of things. And good luck.

About the Author

Alan Klevit is well qualified to talk about art.

Klevit owned and operated four art galleries in the Washington, D.C. Area in the 1970's and '80's, and a wholesale showroom in Los Angeles in the 1980's and '90's. He has been a publisher of fine art, artist's agent, curator of exhibits for galleries, corporate art consultant, art auctioneer, and lecturer/guest speaker. He is also an ardent collector, as well as a music and theater buff.

He has written feature articles for *ART IN AMERICA, ART NEWS, FORECAST MAGAZINE,* and *ART SOURCE,* as well as *THE POTOMAC ALMANAC, GAITHERSBURG GAZETTE* and other newspapers. He has written book reviews for PSYCHOLOGY TODAY and NEW REALITIES magazines. His column, *The Art Beat,* is a regular feature in the *THE MALIBU CHRONICLE,* and has appeared in other newspapers and on line magazines. Klevit also wrote *Three Days in Sedona* [1989]..

Alan had a radio show in Washington, D. C., *Today's Art World with Alan Klevit,* and he hosted two television shows, *Off the Beaten Path* and *The Art Beat,* which aired in the Los Angeles Area. When he is not writing his column or displaying his culinary art skill for his friends, Alan is a frequent guest on local television shows, a sought-after guest art auctioneer for numerous charities throughout the United States, and conducts art auctions and lectures on cruise ships. A charter member of International Fine Art Appraisers, Alan is a recognized expert with a following throughout the art world.